SHARING JESUS' BELIEF IN GOD

Also by Michael Fallon ...

Jesus of Nazareth as portrayed in the New Testament: divine love in a human heart
(Melbourne: Coventry Press, 2020)

The author has written an introductory commentary on all the books of the Old and New Testament. These may be found on the author's website (mbfallon.com).

Once again, Fr Michael has managed to take orthodox Christian understandings – this time on Jesus' belief in God – and offer them in a contemporary context that is easy to understand and applicable to modern readers. Michael has made a significant contribution to the modernising and contextualising of theologies that are otherwise difficult to comprehend. The vision of Jesus presented in this book is a man for the 21st century who can inspire us all to follow in his way.

Alison McKenzie
Alison McKenzie is the current Director
of the Heart of Life Centre for Pastoral and Spiritual Formation in Melbourne.

The drama between belief and unbelief existing in our increasingly secular environment is fuelled by the failure to examine the language we use, The careful research of this remarkable scripture scholar helps to bring new precision to that language.

Monsignor Tony Doherty
Monsignor Tony Doherty has been a leader in Adult Education
in the Archdiocese of Sydney for over fifty years.

Since the mid-70s, my life has been constantly nourished by Michael's wisdom through participating in courses on the scriptures, and pondering the many books he has written over the years.

As I read *Sharing Jesus' Belief in God*, I experienced a call '*to withdraw to a quiet place*'. I felt this book was not to be read from cover to cover, but its wisdom to be pondered deeply in the spirit of John's words '*If you make my word your home you will indeed by my disciples, you will learn the truth and the truth will make you free*' (10:31-32). Michael explores the Word from various perspectives, both affirming our understanding and drawing us to new frontiers.

Paul tells us 'we are God's work of art' (Ephesians 2:10). I sensed a call to nourish this 'work of art', '*to live the good life as from the beginning he had meant us to live it*'. In doing this, may we experience Jesus' promise '*I have come that you may have life and have it to the full*' (John 10:10). It was these words which kept echoing in my heart as I pondered Michael's wisdom.

May *Sharing Jesus' Belief in God* be a source of life, love and commitment for all who read it.

Leone Pallisier OSU
Sr Leone Pallisier OSU was the Leader of the Ursuline Sisters in Australia
and continues to gather women together to explore their faith.

SHARING JESUS' BELIEF IN GOD

MICHAEL FALLON MSC

Published in Australia by
Coventry Press
33 Scoresby Road
Bayswater VIC 3153

ISBN 9781922589576

Copyright © Michael Fallon MSC 2024

All rights reserved. Other than for the purposes and subject to the conditions prescribed under the *Copyright Act*, no part of this publication may be reproduced, stored in a retrieval system, or transmitted in any form or by any means, electronic, mechanical, photocopying, recording or otherwise, without the prior permission of the publisher.

Scripture quotations are the author's own translations.

Nihil Obstat:	Monsignor Peter J. Kenny STD.
	Diocesan Censor
Imprimatur:	Very Reverend Anthony Kerin JCL VG
	Vicar General
	Archdiocese of Melbourne
Date:	13 September 2024

The *Nihil Obstat* and *Imprimatur* are official declarations that a book or pamphlet is free of doctrinal or moral error. No implication is contained therein that those who have granted the Nihil Obstat and Imprimatur agree with the contents, opinions or statements expressed. They do not necessarily signify that the work is approved as a basic text for catechetical instruction.

Catalogue-in-Publication entry is available from the National Library of Australia
http://catalogue.nla.gov.au

Cover design by Ian James – www.jgd.com.au
Text design by Coventry Press
Set in EB Garamond

Printed in Australia

I dedicated this book to Lindsay Peters
in gratitude for friendship
and the stimulation of a shared searching for truth.

Contents

Part One	Setting the Scene	1
1.	Focus on the New Testament	1
2.	Choosing not to believe in God	2
3.	Invitation to explore experience	3
Part Two	Believing in God	7
1.	Knowing and Believing	7
2.	Believing in God	8
Part Three	Israel's faith in God	11
1.	Moses	11
2.	False gods	12
3.	Exile in Babylon	13
4.	Book of Genesis	15
5.	Israel's Prophets	18
6.	Images of God in Israel's sacred texts	18
	• God the Redeemer	18
	• God is compassionate and gracious	19
	• A key response to this compassionate God is longing	21
	• Israel is God's chosen people	22
	• Israel's enemies thought to be God's enemies	23
	• A controlling, intervening God	24
Part Four	Jesus' faith in God	27
1.	Jesus is a member of the human race, like us in everything except sin	27
2.	Jesus' experience of God in nature	32
3.	Jesus' baptismal experience	35
4.	Jesus' concept of God revealed in his teaching and actions	37
5.	Jesus' God is full of compassion	40
6.	Jesus' God does not have enemies	40
7.	Jesus' God is not a controlling, intervening, God	41
8.	Jesus' dying	45

Part Five Divine love in a human heart	49
1. What Jesus revealed continued after his death	49
2. Jesus is God's perfect human word	50
3. Jesus is God with us	53
4. The Trinity	57
5. Misunderstanding the relationship of Jesus and God	65
Part Six Sharing Jesus' faith	71
1. Jesus' faith	71
2. Experiencing love is experiencing God	74
3. Coming to know God	75
4. Of his fulness we have all received	76
Psalm 67:1	78
Saint Anselm: Archbishop of Canterbury (d.1109)	80
Paul to the Galatians 2:20	81

Note: The Bible translations throughout the book are my own.

Part One
Setting the Scene

Dear Reader, it seems to me that I have been engaged in writing this book on 'God' over many decades as I have been attempting to explore and explain the foundational texts of Judaism and Christianity, and, more recently, Islam (see my website: mbfallon.com). Because I am interested in God as revealed by Jesus, I will be constantly referring to the Jewish sacred writings and to the Christian scriptures. The images of God found in the Qur'an lie outside the scope of this book.

1. Focus on the New Testament

In 1987, I published *Who is Jesus? Exploring the responses of the first Christian communities and the early Church Councils* (Parish Ministry Publications; out of print). In 2020, I published *Jesus of Nazareth as portrayed in the New Testament: divine love in a human heart* (Coventry Press). In limiting myself to the New Testament, I realised that I was by-passing the rich reflections of the theologians of the early Church and the wisdom of the early Church Councils. However, accepting that limitation, I judged there was a special value in focusing just on the New Testament.

In offering this book, I am making the same judgment. In seeking to deepen our Christian understanding of God we have two thousand years of rich Christian tradition to draw on. My aim here is to focus on the New Testament: on how the authors portray God as experienced and revealed by Jesus, and how we are graced to share Jesus' faith.

It is refreshing to go back before the important and necessary, but at times abstract language of the early Greek Councils. The language of the New Testament is certainly not abstract. Paul's letters take us into the heart of the early Christian communities to whom they are addressed.

The language of the gospels is liturgical. The gospels are not created as a record of past events. They set out to recall significant experiences, and to celebrate them in order to inspire faith in the assembly by helping to alert us to the significance of past experiences to our present lives. Following the teaching example set by Jesus, they do this especially through story. We are meant to let the story capture our imagination and exercise its power by engaging our mind and heart. Central to the Christian liturgy is celebrating God's faithful love for Jesus, and through him for us all.

2. Choosing not to believe in God

It seems to me that, increasingly, thoughtful adults are opting to see themselves as not believing in God. No doubt there are many reasons for this. I think it is largely because the idea of a personal God does not seem relevant to their lives. The wonderful success of science can tempt us to want the same level of clarity and certainty in our understanding of 'God' as we strive for this in our understanding of the universe, and – when we can't find this – we may choose the path of atheism. The obvious difficulty with this is that ultimately science deals with objects that we can experience, check and measure. 'God' is not such an object. There is more to human experience than can be established by science.

There are scientists who see the universe as 'sacred'. They avoid speaking of 'God', largely because of the way many people tend to imagine 'God'. If we are going to continue speaking of 'God', we must recognise that 'God' is not a separate being, another person. 'God', as philosophers understand, and as we are using the word throughout this book, is the heart of everything and transcends everything, creating everything and sustaining everything in existence. The universe is, indeed, sacred. Science is more at home with words like 'energy', 'force'. The importance of choosing to speak of 'God' rather than using impersonal language is that it reminds us that, while God is not another being, another person, we can relate to the Gracious Mystery we call 'God' in a personal way. Jesus did and Christians since have grown to share Jesus' belief. There is a long history of philosophers who argue that, if something exists, there must exist sufficient grounds that make existence possible. If we had in ourselves sufficient reason for existing, we would have always existed. We must look outside ourselves to find a satisfactory explanation of how it is that we exist and continue to exist. Whatever we find, it too does not have in itself sufficient reason for existing. This is true of everything we see or hear or touch. Yet we do exist.

To avoid an endless and necessarily unsatisfactory search, we must posit the existence of a Reality that does not depend for existence on something other, but that has in itself the completely satisfactory explanation for its existence and is the ultimate cause and sustainer of everything that exists. This is the Reality we call 'God'. A study of the history of their arguments is beyond the scope of this book. My focus is on how Jesus thought of and spoke of this Reality, this 'God'.

3. Invitation to explore experience

I begin by inviting you, dear Reader, to join me in reflecting on a common but mysterious aspect of our experience, an aspect highlighted by the word 'God'. In Sanskrit, the oldest extant language of the Indo-European languages to which English belongs, the hard 'g' (*ghu*) speaks of 'calling'; the 'd' speaks of 'the one'. Whoever first coined the word 'God' was speaking of 'the one called', or 'the one calling'. This invites us – when we use the word 'God' – to explore our experience. Many times, we can readily identify who or what it is that we are calling or that is calling us. Here we are exploring the more mysterious experience that gives rise to the word 'God': the experience of calling or being called, not by something or someone that we can directly see or hear or touch, but by a mysterious presence that we experience in the world around us, and in the depths of our own heart. We are drawn to reach beyond who and where we are to experience a deeper communion, a more conscious belonging to whatever it is that we are calling or that is calling us.

I share with you a personal experience in the hope that it might help you to connect with your own memories. It is an experience I had when I was nineteen. I was in a seminary, studying in preparation for ordination to the priesthood, and was devouring a book that spelled out how Saint Thomas Aquinas was explaining how creatures participate in the being of God. It was a cold mid-winter evening. I was sitting under a tulip tree. It had shed its leaves. Its branches were reaching up to the stars. Suddenly I became aware of belonging to the tree and to the stars. Because of where I was and what I was reading, I believed that I was communing with the universe and so with God.

I have been through some dark times, but the conviction that I belong to the universe and so to God has never left me. And it is not just personal. I am convinced that everything, everyone, belongs. The universe is a sacred place. Each of us belongs, and each of us has a contribution to make, a unique gift, a unique way of loving.

Dear Reader, do you sometimes find yourself calling – in agony or ecstasy or in all the in-between feelings – calling, not a specific person, but beyond any specific being, calling in a profound but mysterious way? Do you ever feel yourself being 'called', not by a locatable person, but again in a profound and mysterious way?

This experience is commonly referred to as 'religious'. The word 'religious' derives from the Latin *ligare*, meaning 'to bind', with the prefix re, meaning 'back'. We can be distracted, out of touch with ourselves and with our world. A religious experience is any experience that binds us back to the real. It can be quite mysterious. In a way that is beyond our comprehension, it engages our heart and mind, and we feel real, because we feel drawn to connect to our own heart and to whatever (whoever) it is that is inviting us into communion.

A study of the religions of the world reveals a confusing mass of ways of speaking about this mysterious Presence, this 'God'. One thing is clear: if we are going to speak of 'God', we must speak only with the most profound humility. We must begin with the realisation that no words can fully express a Reality that transcends our necessarily limited comprehension. We must begin also with the conviction that everyone has a contribution to make here: every culture, every thinker, every artist, every lover.

In his book *Does God exist?* (Collins 1980, p. 498), Hans Küng reminds us: 'Talk of God that does not, in the last resort, emerge from silence and lead again into silence does not know with whom it is dealing'.

When we speak of 'God', we must expect to use words that fall short of the truth. This falling short is not the problem. The problem is when we use the word 'God' carelessly, or – what is worse – when we invoke God to side-step being clear where clarity is possible and required. We must learn not to use 'God' to account for any phenomena in the natural world that we don't understand.

Obviously, if we are going to speak of 'God', we will have to use words. It is essential that we recognise the limits of human language to speak of the creating, sustaining, inspiring, gracious mystery. Take, for example, the word 'person'. To say that God is personal is to say that the values included in the word 'personal' can be attributed to 'God'. To say that God is 'impersonal' is to deny these values to 'God'.

At the same time, we must say that God is not a person the way that you, dear Reader, or I am a person. God transcends our notion of 'person'. Perhaps we should speak of God as 'transpersonal' or 'suprapersonal'.

Similarly, for any human value that we attribute to God. There is a danger of thinking of the all-embracing God in an abstract way. As we will see, Jesus saves us from this by addressing God as 'abba' (dear Father). As the word 'God' asserts, God is the infinite mystery that calls me and that I call (*see page 3*).

We who do not have in ourselves the completely satisfactory explanation for our existence give expression to the realisation of our fundamental dependence by speaking of ourselves and everything we see as 'creatures' and using the word 'Creator' of the one we call 'God'. To speak like this is good so long as we do not imagine God as another being outside ourselves and outside 'creation'.

Teilhard de Chardin expresses this well when he speaks of God as the beyond and the heart of everything. The 'beyond' of everything – God transcends everything we experience. The 'heart' of everything – God is present, creating and sustaining contingent reality from within. This is the theme of the book I was reading under the tulip tree that cold winter evening: creatures participate in the being of the Creator.

Part Two
Believing in God

1. Knowing and Believing

In our search for truth, there are many things that we can rightly and confidently claim to know. To acquire knowledge, we must learn to be attentive to what we see and hear and touch, and to our responses.

Being attentive is key, but it is not enough. We will never attain to truth if we jump from experience to experience without engaging our intellect. To acquire knowledge, we must be intelligent: we must ask questions of our experience. What is going on? Why is this happening? What is it telling me about my world, about myself?

Sometimes, the answer to these questions is straightforward, such that we can confidently conclude that we understand (we know) what is happening. Often, our experience is more complex. Less than satisfied, we find ourselves going back to our experience to search for aspects that we may have overlooked, questions that we may have failed to ask.

In other words, to attain truth we must be reasonable. Only by checking in this way can we be confident that what we think of as an insight is truly such. We must keep asking questions till we are satisfied that our understanding is accurate and complete. Only when all relevant questions have been satisfactorily answered can we form a judgment as to the facts. Only then can we truly know.

A careful examination of the process of coming to know alerts us to a fourth imperative: to attain truth we must be responsible. Knowledge has demands. If we are not willing to adjust our behaviour in the light of what we discover we will – if not consciously then unconsciously – avoid questions we should have asked, with the result that we will fail to discover the truth.

Finally, love plays a key role at every step of our searching to know. I am using 'love' here to speak of the engagement of self, the gift of self. We must give ourselves as we attend to our experience, and in the questioning of our intelligence, and the checking of the insights that occur to us.

It is important to note that most of what we claim to know in any field we don't know, we believe. We don't have the time or the skill to check everything for ourselves. In fields of learning, a person has their contribution to make, but we would scarcely make any progress in any field without believing the results of other peoples' investigations.

It is unreasonable to ignore or reject everything we have not personally checked. To believe is a choice, but, if we choose not to believe anything that we have not personally proved, too much human experience is left unexplored.

In his *Method in Theology* (DLT 1972, p. 233), Bernard Lonergan – whose thinking I am following in this section – gives historians as an example of one community of experts. He writes: 'Historians believe in the sense that they depend on one another's critically evaluated work and participate in the ongoing collaboration for the advance of knowledge'. The same can be said for every field of research. This highlights the importance of peer-reviewing which helps the non-expert to distinguish when it is reasonable and helpful to believe and when it is prudent to withhold belief.

2. Believing in God

As regards seeking to know God, everyone suffers from the same limitations: God is not an object of direct experience for anyone in either the outer or the inner world. It follows that no one can know God. If we choose to believe in God, it cannot be because others know God and we trust them. No one can directly experience and come to know God. However, the fact that others choose to believe in God can attract us to choose to believe when we see and are attracted by the fruit of their believing. This choice to believe can be strengthened when we observe the fruit of belief in our own lives. Anselm of Canterbury establishes a key perspective for our search when he writes: 'I do not seek to understand that I might believe. I seek to believe that I might understand' (*Proslogion* online, last words of Chapter One).

Believing can open pathways to truth that would otherwise remain hidden. If we choose to give ourselves to belief in God, we are choosing to live with mystery. We are choosing to bow our heads in adoration of God, and in wonderment at the sacredness of the universe that is constantly coming to be. Believing in God is a response to religious experience: the experience of our person as a gift and the experience of being called, being drawn, inspired, and led. We envisage God, the One we choose to believe exists, as the attracting source of everything that exists.

The key role of belief is beautifully expressed by one of Australia's finest lyric poets, James McAuley. A few weeks before his untimely death from cancer, as the 'springs' of his life were drying up, he wrote:

> I know that faith is like a root that's tough, inert, and old.
> Yet it can send up its green shoot and flower against the cold.
> I know there is a grace that flows when all the springs run dry.
> It wells up to renew the rose and lift the cedars high.

Part Three
Israel's faith in God

1. Moses

In the Books of Exodus, Leviticus, Numbers and Deuteronomy, the focus is on Moses, who is portrayed in such a way as to show how to listen to God, and how to behave in a way that opens us to God's grace.

Moses' communion with God began with a call to go back to Egypt to work to free his people from slavery. The Scriptures picture Moses' encounter with God, an encounter that is necessarily mysterious. The symbol of their encounter is a bush that is on fire but not burning (*Exodus 3:2*). Moses is portrayed as sensing the divine Presence. What is asked of Moses is that he go back to Egypt, trusting that God would be with him.

Moses wants to name God. To name is to claim to know, even to control. Instead of a name God asks Moses to believe that 'I will be who I will be' (*ehyeh asher ehyeh*, *Exodus 3:14*). The word 'Yahweh' is linguistically related to the *ehyeh* of this text. It is not a name. Rather, it holds God's promise to be with Moses when he strives to carry out the mission he believed was given him by God. He will find God present, sustaining him.

The authors of the Book of Exodus share with us their understanding of the intimacy of communion with God. They portray Moses as spending forty days and forty nights on the mountain with God. The climax comes when Moses pleads: 'Show me your glory, I pray' (Exodus 33:18). The text continues: 'Yahweh said, "you cannot see my face; for no one shall see me and live ... See, there is a place by me where you shall stand on the rock; and while my glory passes by I will put you in a cleft of the rock, and I will cover you with my hand until I have passed by; then I will take away my hand, and you shall see my back; but my face shall not be seen'" (*Exodus 33:20-23*). In obeying the Torah, we are obeying God. We are seeing God's 'back' as we follow the path God reveals to us. It is by following the way God leads us on that we enjoy the communion with God for which we long.

The Scriptures of Israel are consistent in asserting that Yahweh, their God, is beyond direct human experience: 'You cannot see my face'.

It is important to realise that transcendence does not mean distance:

> Yahweh, you search me, and you know me.
> You know my resting and my rising.
> You discern my purpose from afar.
> You mark when I walk or lie down.
> All my ways lie open to you ...
> Where can I go from your spirit.
> Where can I flee from your face? (*Psalm 139: 1-3,7*)

2. False gods

Besides the success of science, another phenomenon that helps account for the growth of atheism is the many false gods spruiked by people who see themselves as religious. As I begin my reflections, I realise that what I write could so easily fall into this category. But I want to try to speak of God in words that make sense, while honouring the mystery. Failure in clarity spawns a healthy atheism.

However, it seems to me that when atheism becomes a fixed position, it is tragic. Too much beauty may go unnoticed, too many insights may be missed, too much loving may fail to mature. If we avoid being fixed, if we remain open, a greater awareness of beauty may lead us to a sense of the presence in our lives of the Gracious Mystery we call 'God'. An experience of mature loving may lead us to a sense of the sacredness of love itself. My aim in this book is highly ambitious. I want to speak of God only in words that make sense because, while necessarily limited, the words are clear and defensible. I'll give it my best shot. It is you, dear Reader, who will know whether I am adding to the confusion or helping contribute to our shared search.

3. Exile in Babylon

At the time of the destruction of Jerusalem and the Exile in Babylon, some six hundred years before the birth of Jesus, the people of Judah had a rich heritage of scrolls, including what they judged to be the inspired words of the prophets Amos, Hosea, Isaiah and Micah, as well as early versions of material that focused on Moses and the origins of Israel's religion. They also had a rich oral tradition of stories from the various local sanctuaries in Judah and from a number of sanctuaries in Israel, stories that were brought south by refugees escaping the Assyrian invasion in the late eighth century before Christ (c.721 BC).

The presence of the temple in Jerusalem gave the people of Judah a confident expectation that God would not allow Judah to suffer the fate of Israel. They were wrong. In 598 BC, the Babylonian army starved Jerusalem into surrender. Everyone who was judged useful by the Babylonian leaders was carted off into exile in Babylon. They took their precious scrolls with them.

The biggest shock the exiles experienced in Babylon was witnessing what to them was the shallowness of the Babylonian images and cult of the gods. As we reflect on the false gods experienced by the exiles in Babylon, it is up to us to discern the false gods that we experience. In so many ways, the Babylonian culture was superior to that of Judah, but not when it comes to religion. The contrast between the God of Israel and the gods of Babylon is expressed powerfully in Psalm 115.

> Our God is in the heavens; he does whatever he pleases.
> Their idols are silver and gold, the work of human hands.
> They have mouths, but do not speak; eyes, but do not see.
> They have ears, but do not hear; noses, but do not smell.
> They have hands, but do not feel; feet, but do not walk.
> They make no sound in their throats.
> Those who make them are like them; so are all who trust in them.
>
> *(Psalm 115:3-8)*

We find the same sentiment expressed in the following, composed during the exile, and incorporated into the Isaiah scroll (*Isaiah 44:12-20*):

> The ironsmith fashions it and works it over the coals, shaping it with hammers, and forging it with his strong arm ... The carpenter stretches a line, marks it out with a stylus, fashions it with planes, and marks it with a compass; he makes it in human form, with human beauty, to be set up in a shrine. He cuts down cedars or chooses a holm tree or an oak and lets it grow strong among the trees of the forest. He plants a cedar, and the rain nourishes it. Then it can be used as fuel. Part of it he takes and warms himself; he kindles a fire and bakes bread. Then he makes a god and worships it, makes it a carved image, and bows down before it. Half of it he burns in the fire; over this half he roasts meat, eats it, and is satisfied. He also warms himself and says, 'Ah, I am warm, I can feel the fire!' The rest of it he makes into a god, his idol, bows down to it and worships it; he prays to it and says, 'Save me, for you are my god!'.

It can be argued that the exiles misunderstood the Babylonian cult. The Babylonians were not worshipping the idols. They were worshipping what they imagined to be the invisible gods portrayed by the idols. The idols can be compared to the cherubim on the mercy seat in the inner sanctuary of the Jewish temple. The Judahites were not worshipping the cherubim.

The contrast between the religious cult of Babylon and that of Judah is expressed later in the Isaiah scroll.

> Listen to me, O house of Jacob, all the remnant of the house of Israel, who have been borne by me from your birth, carried from the womb. Even to your old age I am he, even when you turn grey, I will carry you. I have made, and I will bear; I will carry and will save. To whom will you liken me and make me equal, and compare me, as though we were alike?
> (*Isaiah 46:3-5*)

Experiencing the poverty of the Babylonian images of God, the exiles realised the incomparable superiority of their God, Yahweh:

> I am Yahweh your God, who brought you out of the land of Egypt, out of the house of slavery; you shall have no other gods before me. You shall not have strange gods before me.
> *(Exodus 20:1-3)*

They went further, even denying the existence of other so-called gods:

> I am Yahweh, and there is no other.
>   Besides me there is no god
> I arm you, though you do not know me,
>   so that they may know, from the rising of the sun,
>   and from the west, that there is no one besides me.
> I am Yahweh, and there is no other. (Isaiah 45:5-7)

4. Book of Genesis

It was probably their witnessing the Babylonian cult that inspired the authors of the opening chapters of the Book of Genesis to express in writing what they saw as their far-superior understanding of God the Creator. It is essential to grasp that the language of Genesis 1 to 11 is cultic, and so dramatic and poetic.

As already noted of the New Testament gospels (see '*Focus on the New Testament*, page 1'), the texts of the Old Testament are not created as a record of past events. They set out to recall significant experiences, and to celebrate them in order to inspire faith in the assembly by helping to alert them to the significance of past experiences to their present lives.

They do this especially through story. We are meant to let the story capture our imagination and exercise its power by engaging our mind and heart. Central to the biblical scrolls is celebrating God's faithful love. We fail to understand the depth of the truths this literature is conveying if we read it as recording historical facts.

The authors of Genesis are sharing their faith that everything we see and touch expresses – in a limited but real way – something of the mysterious God who brings creation into being and sustains it in existence. In the Genesis story, the 'beginning' occurred when a 'Spirit from God swept over the face of the waters' (*Genesis 1:2*). God's Spirit is the love that we know in the world around us and in our response. It is the Spirit that enables creation to enjoy communion with the Creator. It is the Spirit that is the loving, life-sustaining, energy that flows from the Creator to the creature, and that carries our response as creatures back to our Creator.

The Book of Genesis begins with Israel's God, Yahweh, creating the observable universe, sustaining it in existence and declaring it good. Everything we see is an expression of God's Being, expressed in God's Word ('Let there be ...), and inspired by God's Spirit. In the Genesis narrative, God's creating reaches its climax with the creation of the human race, and God's giving human beings as man and woman the power to continue God's creating of the human race. The Genesis text tells us that it is Yahweh, Israel's God, who wanted man and woman to enjoy each other and to enjoy communion with God in a paradise, a walled garden with fountains and fruit trees. Creation is declared to be 'very good' (*Genesis 1:31*).

This is how the authors of Genesis understood God's intention in creating. It was obvious to them that we are not living in a paradise. So, what went wrong? What God intended as a paradise is often experienced as a wasteland. Childbearing is painful. All is not right between the sexes. Shepherds and farmers fight over the limited supply of water. When tribes meet, instead of harmony there is often violence. Today, we are confronted with the destructive power of global warming, and the possibility of nuclear war which puts everything at risk. What has gone wrong?

There is no simple answer, but the key insight expressed in Genesis is that the problem arises when human beings are not content to remain open to God's love – God's Self-gift. We want to run our own lives. We want to decide what is good and what is evil. We want to be 'like God' (Genesis 3:5) as an achievement of our own efforts. We want to decide for ourselves what is good and what is evil. Instead of waiting for and welcoming the harvest, we want to reach up and snatch the fruit.

The problem is sin: instead of listening to God's word – and God speaks to us through creation – instead of being open to God's Spirit – and God's Spirit is moving our hearts and minds – we proudly and foolishly determine to be independent.

As the drama unfolds, we recognise every man, including ourselves, in Adam and his behaviour. We recognise every woman, including ourselves, in Eve. It is a misreading of Genesis as a record of historical events that gave rise to the idea of a Fall, and our inheriting a fallen nature. The Genesis text is not an account of historical events. It is not claiming as an historical fact that human beings first lived in a paradise, and then, because they sinned, they were cast out of the garden. On the contrary, the Genesis account describes in dramatic poetry God's loving intent and the authors' understanding of why our experience is so different from what God intended in creating.

Paradise is how the authors of Genesis pictured God wanting us to live: 'walking with God in the garden at the time of the evening breeze' (*Genesis 3:8*). We are created for communion with God. When that communion is broken the universe is in danger of reverting to chaos. This destruction is symbolised by a universal flood – an image borrowed from Babylon (see the *Epic of Gilgamesh*).

According to the dramatic version of the Genesis account, all would have been destroyed except for the faith and obedience of Noah. He listens to God. He obeys God's Word. He is inspired by God's Spirit. He builds a temple (not a boat) that rises above the flood, and, when the flood finally subsides, out of this temple come all the living beings that can renew creation. There is still sin in this renewed creation, but there is also a hunger for communion, and there are people, like Noah, who encourage us to believe that communion with God is still possible. We might be tempted to be unfaithful, but God remains faithful, and that is the source of our hope.

In Genesis 12 to 50, we have a record of ancient stories handed down orally from generation to generation. Sin still haunts the people of Israel, but the lives of the tribal patriarchs are portrayed as examples of obedience to God. God remains mysteriously transcendent, but we can come to some understanding of how God works in our world through the example of Abraham, Isaac, Jacob and Joseph.

5. Israel's Prophets

In the writings, beginning with the final years of the eighth century BC, we witness the disobedience described in the drama of the Garden of Eden. We also witness the example and encouragement of prophetic figures who call us to exercise the freedom God gives us to embrace God's gift. There is Amos, Hosea, Isaiah and Micah in the eighth century; Zephaniah, Nahum, Habakkuk and Jeremiah in the seventh century; Ezekiel, Haggai and Zephaniah in the sixth century; Obadiah, Joel, Malachi and Jonah in the fifth century, as well as the unnamed people who lived holy lives, including those who kept reflecting on and updating the ancient scrolls.

6. Images of God in Israel's sacred texts

From people's experience of need, of wonder, of success and failure, of sin, but also of being cared for and loved, the Jewish Scriptures projected onto God a mixture of sometimes conflicting characteristics.

• God the Redeemer

For the Jewish people, God was the one who liberated from slavery in Egypt. Consistent with this was their confidence in looking to God as a liberator. God's creating and sustaining grace is present, working against pressures from outside or from within that hinder a creature from being what it is and from becoming what it is growing to be.

> Draw near to me, Yahweh, redeem me, set me free. (*Psalm 69:18*)

> Some sat in darkness and gloom, prisoners in misery and chains. Weighed down by the burdens of their misery, they collapsed with no one to help them. Then they cried out to you, O God, and you came to their rescue, breaking their fetters and dispersing the gloom. You lift up the needy from their distress, shepherding them like a flock. (*Psalm 107:10-14, 41*)

> Turn to me, Yahweh, and be gracious to me ... free me from oppression. (*Psalm 119:132, 134*).

> Yahweh sets the prisoners free. (Psalm 146:7)

• God is compassionate and gracious

Moses was on the mountain forty days and forty nights. He longed to see God. God told him that that is not possible. God invited Moses to stand on the rock. God would pass by but would cover Moses' eyes to stop Moses from seeing him. As he passed, he cried in words that are repeated throughout the Jewish Scriptures.

> Yahweh, Yahweh, a God tenderly compassionate and gracious, long-suffering and abounding in steadfast love and faithfulness, forgiving iniquity, transgression and sin. (*Exodus 34:6-7*)

At the heart of ancient Israel's identity is the conviction that God is present and active in their lives. They believed that it was their God, Yahweh, who raised up Moses to liberate them from slavery in Egypt. They believed that it is Yahweh who led them through the desert, formed them into a people, and made a home for them in Canaan.

Belief in God's loving presence and action in their lives is at the heart of the identity of the ancient Israelites. This creed is found throughout the Bible.

Who is a God like you, pardoning iniquity and passing over the transgression of the remnant of your possession? You delight in showing steadfast love. You will again have compassion upon us; you will tread our iniquities under foot. You will cast all our sins into the depths of the sea. You will show faithfulness to Jacob and steadfast love to Abraham, as you have sworn to our ancestors from the days of old. (*Micah 7:18-20*)

God will be tenderly compassionate according to the abundance of his steadfast love. (*Lamentations 3:32*)

Yahweh your God is gracious and merciful and will not turn away his face from you. (*2 Chronicles 30:9*)

You are a God ready to forgive, gracious and tenderly compassionate, long-suffering and abounding in steadfast love. You did not forsake our ancestors. (*Nehemiah 9:17*)

I know that you are a gracious God, merciful, long suffering, and abounding in steadfast love (*Jonah 4:2*)

You, Yahweh, are a God tenderly compassionate and gracious, long suffering and abounding in steadfast love and faithfulness. (*Psalm 86:15*)

Glorious and majestic are the deeds of God, whose justice endures forever. Who can fail to acclaim God's wonderful deeds? God is gracious and tenderly compassionate. (*Psalm 111:3-4*)

God is gracious and tenderly compassionate, long-suffering, abounding in covenant love. God is good to all, tenderly compassionate to all creation. (*Psalm 145:8-9*)

Yahweh surrounds you with steadfast love and tender compassion so that your youth is renewed like an eagle's. He made known his ways to Moses, his acts to the people of Israel. Yahweh is tenderly compassionate and gracious, long-suffering and abounding in steadfast love. As a father has compassion for his children, so Yahweh has compassion for those who revere him. For he knows how we are; he remembers that we are dust. The steadfast love of Yahweh always was and always will be for those who revere him, and his righteousness passes on from children to grandchildren. (*Psalm 103:4-17*)

• A key response to this compassionate God is longing

Consistent with this conviction of God being present and active in their lives is their profound longing to carry out their side of the covenant, by discerning what it is that God wants them to do – a longing that fills their psalms and their cult. Accompanying this longing is a profound sense of wonder, thanksgiving and praise.

The psalmist knows the longing experienced by Moses: Show me your glory, I pray. (*Exodus 33:18*)

> I wait for you, I long for you, O God. I count on your word.
> I am longing for you more than the watchman for daybreak.
> (*Psalm 130:5-6*)

> O God, you hear the longing of the poor. You listen to them and strengthen their hearts. (*Psalm 17:10*)

> Your voice within me says: 'Come, seek my face'. It is your face that my heart seeks. (*Psalm 27:8*)

> The upright shall behold his face. (*Psalm 11:7*)

> One thing I ask of God, this is what I seek: to behold God's beauty. (*Psalm 27:4*)

It is by listening obediently to God that we will enjoy the communion we long for.

> The law of Yahweh is perfect, reviving the soul;
> the decrees of Yahweh are sure, making wise the simple;
> the precepts of Yahweh are right, rejoicing the heart;
> the commandment of Yahweh is clear, enlightening the eyes;
> reverence for Yahweh is pure, enduring forever;
> the ordinances of Yahweh are true and righteous altogether.
> They are more to be desired than gold;
> sweeter also than honey, and drippings of the honeycomb.
> (*Psalm 19:7-10*)

• Israel is God's chosen people

Another image that is basic in the portrayal of God that we find in the Jewish Scriptures witnesses to the belief of the ancient people of Israel that they are God's chosen people.

> If you obey my voice and keep my covenant, you shall be my treasured possession out of all the peoples. (*Exodus 19:5*)

> Yahweh, your God, has chosen you out of all the peoples on earth to be his people, his treasured possession. (*Deuteronomy 7:6*)

> It is you Yahweh has chosen out of all the people on earth to be his people, his treasured possession. (*Deuteronomy 14:2*)

> Today Yahweh has obtained your agreement to be his treasured people. (*Deuteronomy 26:18*)

> They shall be mine, says Yahweh of hosts, my special possession. (*Malachi 3:17*)

This special place for Israel as portrayed in the Jewish Scriptures is highlighted by the authors of Genesis in their portrayal of the patriarch Abraham. God calls him and promises: 'I will make of you a great nation, and I will bless you, and make your name great, so that you will be a blessing' (*Genesis 12:2*).

God is pictured as promising Abraham: 'Look toward heaven and count the stars if you can count them. So shall your descendants be' (*Genesis 15:5-6*).

This is my covenant with you: You shall be the ancestor of a multitude of nations. (*Genesis 17:4*)

It is evident that the people of ancient Israel embraced the idea that they were God's chosen people. However, that Abraham is called to be the father 'of a multitude of nations' hardly features in the ancient accounts. Psalm 87 is an exception:

> Zion is established on the holy mountain cherished by God. Glorious things are spoken of you, O city of God. Egypt and Babylon I will count among her citizens. Philistia, Tyre

and Ethiopia are registered among her children. Zion will be called 'mother', for all will be her children. While they dance, they will sing 'in you all find their home'.

So challenging is this idea that those responsible for translating the Hebrew text of Psalm 87 into Aramaic, the language of the people, radically altered the text:

> Blessed be my people whom I brought out of Egypt. Because they sinned before me, I carried them into exile to Assyria, but now that they have repented, they shall be my people and my inheritance, even Israel.

• Israel's enemies thought to be God's enemies

The sense of being especially loved by God, is, of course, quite beautiful. The problem is that the ancient Israelites thought that, since they were especially chosen by God, their enemies must be God's enemies.

> The enemy is destroyed, memory of them has perished. You, Yahweh, razed to the ground their cities. (*Psalm 9:6*)

They understand that they are expected to 'despise those not approved by God' (*Psalm 15:3*).

They appeal to God: 'Destroy the offspring of your enemies from the earth' (*Psalm 21:10*).

> Annihilate the nations in your wrath, that they may be no more; that they may know that God rules in Jacob and to the utmost ends of the earth. (*Psalm 59:13*)

Psalm 68 portrays God as a Warrior Lord who gallops over the plain and 'scatters the enemy' (*Psalm 68:1*). God shatters the heads of his enemies' (*Psalm 68:21*). The people of Israel are challenged 'to bathe their enemy's feet in blood, that the tongues of our dogs may have their share of the foe' (*Psalm 68:23*).

'It is God who judges the nations, shattering heads, heaping up corpses' (*Psalm 110:6*).

Addressing Babylon, the psalmist is confident God will ensure that 'Blessed and happy will they be who take your children and dash them against the rock' (*Psalm 137:9*).

• A controlling, intervening God

It is one thing to experience; it is another to interpret the meaning of experience. The image of God in ancient Israel, born of their understanding of their experience, is complicated by their way of attributing power to God, ultimately their understanding of power as control. Since they thought of God as all-powerful, they assumed that whatever actually happens must be either directly intending by God or permitted as a means of God achieving God's will.

Instead of keeping their focus on the Gracious Mystery in their history and in their lives, they thought of God as intervening in response to their behaviour, blessing them when they obeyed God's will and punishing them when they failed to obey. When they suffered drought, or were defeated in battle, or when Jerusalem was destroyed by a foreign nation, they jumped to the conclusion that these experiences demonstrated God's anger with them, and that God was punishing them.

The following selection of texts expresses an understanding that permeates their Scriptures.

> Serve God with fear, with trembling kiss God's feet, or God will be angry with you, and you will perish on the way, for God's anger is quickly kindled. (*Psalm 2:12*)
>
> Make them suffer the consequences of their sin, O God. (*Psalm 5:10*)
>
> We are consumed in your anger, overwhelmed by your wrath. All our days wither beneath your glance. Who can grasp the power of your anger? Who appreciates the force of your wrath? (*Psalm 90:7, 9, 11*)

Reflecting on the sins committed by some of Israel's ancestors, the psalmist writes: 'Before they had satisfied their craving, while the food was still in their mouths, God slew the strongest among them, struck down the flower of Israel' (*Psalm 78:30-31*).

This way of thinking about God opened the way to attempts to manipulate, if not to control, God.

It is one thing (and a good thing) to express our needs to God, it is another to try to influence God to meet our needs by intervening in our lives in responding to our cry for help.

God is ever present, ever gracious, ever offering God's Self to creation, ever creating, sustaining, inspiring. Jesus knew this, hence his giving of himself to all; hence his plea that we will love as he loves, as God loves by giving ourselves to others. We are invited to open ourselves to welcome grace, however the largely random energies impact our lives. We are invited to commit ourselves to a trusting belief, tested and enlightened by reason.

When we come in Part Four to look at Jesus, we will note how the idea of ancient Israel that God is a controlling, intervening God had a negative influence upon how Jesus' self-giving on Calvary was portrayed by some theologians. We will also see that God as seen and portrayed by Jesus is not a controlling, intervening God, but a constant, creating and sustaining, Self-giving presence.

Part Four
Jesus' faith in God

1. Jesus is a member of the human race, like us in everything except sin

Before we examine Jesus' belief in God it is necessary that we acknowledge that Jesus of Nazareth is, like us, truly a member of the human race. It is necessary to insist on this because there are people who think of his divinity (his intimate communion with God) as radically changing his humanity. The Letter to the Hebrews says of Jesus: 'He had to become like us his brothers and sisters in every respect' (*Hebrews 4:15*). Since Jesus is human like us, why wouldn't we think that his conception was like ours?

Luke writes: 'The angel Gabriel was sent by God to a town in Galilee called Nazareth, to a virgin betrothed to a man whose name was Joseph, of the house of David. The virgin's name was Mary' (*Luke 1:26-27*). Mary is told that she is to conceive one who 'will be called the Son of the Most High' (*Luke 1:32*). Mary says to the angel, 'How can this be, since I am a virgin?' The angel says to her, 'The Holy Spirit will come upon you, and the power of the Most High will overshadow you; therefore the child to be born will be holy; he will be called Son of God' (*Luke 1:34-35*). In the Apostles' Creed, we declare: 'I believe in Jesus, God's only Son, who was conceived by the Holy Spirit, born of the virgin Mary'. We need to ask: 'what is Luke asserting?'

The first point to make is that Luke is asserting that Jesus is the 'Son of God' – a teaching that recurs throughout Luke's Gospel and Acts; indeed, throughout the whole of the New Testament. In his account of Jesus' baptism, Luke states: 'A voice came from heaven: You are my Son, the Beloved; with you I am well pleased'

(*Luke 3:22*). Likewise in his account of Jesus' transfiguration on Mount Tabor, the three disciples hear God declare: 'This my Son, the Chosen; listen to him' (*Luke 9:35*). Jesus prays: 'All things have been handed over to me by my Father; and no one knows who the Son is except the Father, or who the Father is except the Son and anyone to whom the Son chooses to reveal him' (*Luke 10:22*).

In a parable referring to himself as sent by God, Jesus states: 'The owner of the vineyard said, What shall I do? I will send my beloved son; surely they will respect him' (*Luke 20:13*).

After describing Paul's enlightenment on the road to Damascus, Luke states 'immediately Saul began to proclaim Jesus in the synagogues, saying, 'He is the Son of God' (*Acts 9:20*).

We find the same teaching in Luke's teacher, Paul. A few examples should suffice. Paul writes: 'God revealed God's Son to me, so that I might proclaim him among the Gentiles' (*Galatians 1:16*). 'I live by the faith of the Son of God, loving me, giving himself for me' (*Galatians 2:20*). 'When the fulness of time had come, God sent his Son, born of a woman' (*Galatians 4:4*). 'God is faithful; by him you were called into the communion of God's Son, Jesus the Messiah, our Lord' (*1 Corinthians 1:9*). 'God has rescued us from the power of darkness and transferred us into the kingdom of his beloved Son' (*Colossians 1:13*). 'The Son of God, Jesus the Messiah, whom we proclaimed among you, was not "Yes and No"; in him it is always "Yes"' (*2 Corinthians 1:19*).

In the opening words of his Letter to the churches in Rome, Paul introduces himself: 'Paul, a servant of Jesus the Messiah, called to be an apostle, set apart for the gospel of God, which he promised beforehand through his prophets in the holy scriptures, the gospel concerning God's Son, who was descended from David according to the flesh and was declared to be Son of God with power according to the spirit of holiness by resurrection from the dead, Jesus the Messiah, our Lord' (*Romans 1:1-4*). Later in the same letter, we read: 'I serve God with my spirit by announcing the gospel of God's Son' (*Romans 1:9*). 'We were reconciled to God through the death of God's Son' (*Romans 5:10*).

The first thing that Luke is asserting in the Prologue of his Gospel is that Jesus is the Son of God.

Luke's second point is that Jesus was conceived by the Holy Spirit. This is also at the heart of Christian faith. From his conception, Jesus is open to the intimate communion that God is offering him. It is to this intimate communion that we refer when we speak of the Holy Spirit.

Thirdly, Luke's account has something to say about Jesus' mother: she is a virgin. Does this mean that God miraculously intervened, bypassing Joseph, and enabling Mary to conceive Jesus while remaining physically a virgin? This is how Christians have traditionally understood it. Is that what Luke is asserting? It is important that faith seeks understanding. This must be a humble seeking for we are dealing with matters that concern God, and so are mysterious.

Our faith that Jesus is God's Son is not dependent on Mary's physical virginity. When we speak of God as Jesus' Father, we are asserting that everything that Jesus is, and everything he says and does comes from God. We are not speaking of biological paternity.

In the rest of the Prologue and throughout his Gospel and Acts, Luke does not refer again to Mary as a virgin. It is only stated here in Luke 1:26-35. Later in his Prologue, we are told: 'the child's father and mother were amazed' at what Simeon was saying about the child Jesus (*Luke 2:13*). We are told that 'every year Jesus' parents went to Jerusalem for the festival of the Passover' (*Luke 2:41*). Jesus went with them but went missing. Luke writes that when 'his parents found him, his mother said to him: Child, why have you treated us like this? Look your father and I have been searching for you with great anxiety' (*Luke 2:48*). None of these texts leave us with the impression that Jesus' family life was radically unlike ours.

Another factor to consider is that Luke's Prologue introduces the reader to key theological assertions that are central to his presentation of Jesus in his Gospel. Its focus is not on biography.

Luke's powerful stories prepare the reader for his interpretive commentary.

Furthermore, again and again, the New Testament speaks of Jesus as 'the Son of God', but Mary's virginity is never mentioned by Mark, never mentioned in the Gospel of the Beloved Disciple, never mentioned by Paul in any of his letters. We find no mention of it in any of the other letters in the New Testament, or in the Apocalypse. Jesus being the Son of God is at the heart of the teaching of the New Testament. We cannot claim the same for Mary's virginity.

To understand Luke's purpose in presenting Mary as a virgin we need to examine the thinking of those for whom he is writing. Luke's readers were familiar with legends that stated that the founders of the great cities of the Greco-Roman world had a god for their father and a virgin for their mother. Romulus and Remus are celebrated as twin brothers, the sons of a vestal virgin named Rhea Silvia and the god Mars. Asclepius was the son of Apollo. His mother was the virgin Coronis. Helen was the daughter of Zeus and Leda. Alexander, the Ptolemies, and the Caesars were said to have been 'virgin-born'. Is Luke speaking of Mary as a virgin to state – using language that his readers would understand – that it is Jesus who is divine (the Son of God), not the heroes of their myths, or their emperors?

Virgil (70-19BC) writes that shepherds heralded Augustus's birth. His birth is called 'good news' ('evangelion'). Augustus, the new-born child, is proclaimed saviour (soter) and described as lord (kyrios). He is seen as the bringer of a new age of peace. He is called the son of God. He shows exceptional qualities at the age of twelve, and so it goes on. In his *Lives of the Caesars*, Suetonius (69-122AD) says that there were prophecies and portents before the birth of Augustus, whose conception was miraculous. It took place in the context of worship at a temple. Upon his birth, Augustus was declared to be a King and a Ruler. Luke mentions Augustus (*Luke 2:1*) to tell his readers to look to Jesus, not Augustus, as their 'saviour' and 'peacemaker'.

There is one other place where Mary is called a virgin. It is in the Gospel of Matthew, but, once again, it is only in the Prologue of his Gospel, not in the body of the Gospel. Commenting on Matthew's prologue, Ulrich Luz writes: 'We do not need to assume that this story, which strongly follows traditional schemas, contains information from the circle of Jesus' family. Nor are the signs favourable for the historicity of the virgin birth, which in the New Testament is transmitted only by Matthew and Luke ... It is probably part of the attempt of Jewish Christian communities to bear witness to Jesus who was appointed by God as Son according to the Spirit (*Romans 1:4*) in a way that was analogous to other ancient stories in the form of an infancy narrative. The virgin birth then is a means of confessing faith and has no historical background' (Ulrich Luz: *Commentary on Matthew*, Fortress Press 2007, volume I, page 93). The author of the Letter to the Hebrews writes: 'Jesus had to become like his brothers and sisters in every respect' (*Hebrews 2:17*). 'We have a high priest who in every respect has been tested as we are, yet without sin' (Hebrews 4:15). This is picked up in the teaching of the Second Vatican Council: 'The Son of God worked with human hands, thought with a human mind, acted with a human will, and loved with a human heart. He has truly been made one of us, like to us in all things except sin' (*The Church in the Modern World* (*Gaudium et Spes*) n. 22, para 2).

In portraying Mary as a virgin in language familiar to his audience, Luke reinforces his focus on God as Jesus' 'Father', and on Jesus' intimacy with the one he called 'Abba'. Luke's scene of the virginal conception is also a beautiful way of portraying the special relationship between Mary and God. A virgin is a person who gives his or her first love to another. Mary's first love was for God, and the conception of Jesus was a fruit of that special love. Would that every conception came from such a communion. In his Commentary on Luke in the *Hermeneia* Series 2002 (volume 1, page 45) François Bovon writes: 'Biblical marriages are sometimes spiritualised in the Hellenistic Judaism of Egypt, where sexual vocabulary is applied to the mystical union with God. In Philo it becomes clear that births like that of Isaac were regarded as virgin births; for Philo himself these are only an allegory of the ecstatic union of the soul with God'.

In repeating Luke's description of Mary as a virgin, is the Christian community (however it has imagined this over the centuries) been keeping before us the intimate relationship between Jesus and the God he called 'Abba'; a communion that we speak of when we refer to the Holy Spirit?

2. Jesus' experience of God in nature

When Jesus gazed at the fields, the woods, and the lake he would have been at home with Israel's creed and with the psalmist's prayer: 'I am filled with awe at your presence' (*Psalm 5:7*).

Those who live at earth's farthest bounds are awed by your signs.
You make the gateways of the morning and the evening
    shout for joy.
You visit the earth and water it. You greatly enrich it.
The river of God is full of water.
You provide the people with grain,
for so you have prepared it.
You water its furrows abundantly, settling its ridges,
softening it with showers, and blessing its growth.
You crown the year with your bounty,
your wagon tracks overflow with richness.
The pastures of the wilderness overflow,
the hills gird themselves with joy,
the meadows clothe themselves with flocks,
the valleys deck themselves with grain.
They shout and sing together for joy. (*Psalm 65:8-13*)

How often did he pray as he gazed at the heavens:

The heavens are telling the glory of God,
and the firmament proclaims his handiwork.
Day to day pours forth speech,
and night to night declares knowledge.

There is no speech, nor are there words: their voice is not heard,
yet it goes out through all the earth,
and their words to the end of the world.
In the heavens he has set a tent for the sun,
which comes out like a bridegroom from his wedding canopy,
and like a strong man runs its course with joy. (Psalm 19:1-6)

When I look at the heavens, the work of your hands,
the moon and the stars that you have set in place,
what am I, a mortal human being, that you are mindful of me,
that you care for me? (*Psalm 8:8*)

We can picture Jesus singing:

Your presence fills me with joy. (*Psalm 16:11*)

It is you, O God, who light my lamp.
It is you who light up my darkness. (*Psalm 18:28*)

I am continually with you; you hold my right hand.
You guide me with your counsel,
  and afterward you will receive me with honour.
Whom have I in heaven but you?
There is nothing on earth that I desire other than you.
My flesh and my heart may fail, but God is the strength of my heart,
  and my portion forever.
For me it is good to be near God. (*Psalm 73:23-28*)

The voice of Yahweh flashes forth flames of fire.
The voice of Yahweh shakes the wilderness;
  the Lord shakes the wilderness of Kadesh.
The voice of Yahweh causes the oaks to whirl
  and strips the forest bare. (*Psalm 29:7-9*)

Thunder and lightning we can experience. We don't directly experience God. The psalmist gives expression to those who sense the sacredness of nature, the mysterious Presence of a transcendent, yet immanent, God, calling to them from the heart of creation. In hearing the thunder, the psalmist is hearing what he believes to be the voice of God.

As he walked with his father to Sepphoris, Jesus witnessed shepherds watching over the flocks. He could pray with the psalmist:

> You, O God, are my shepherd, I shall not want.
> You make me lie down in green pastures.
> You lead me beside still waters.
> You restore my soul. (*Psalm 23:1-2*)

He could not go into the woods near Nazareth without encountering a deer. It is easy to picture him singing the following psalms learned in the synagogue:

> As the deer yearns for running streams,
> so my whole being longs for you, my God.
> With all the yearning of my soul I thirst for God.
> When, O God, will I come to see your face? (*Psalm 42:1*)

> O God, you are my God, for you I rise at dawn
> I thirst for you, my body pines for you,
> like a dry, weary, waterless land. (*Psalm 63:1*)

When Jesus observed a bird protecting its young, he could hear God speaking to him with the psalmist:

> God will cover you as a bird covers its young.
> God's wings will shelter you. (*Psalm 91:4*)

We can picture Jesus calling on his memories to pray with the psalmist:

> I am like a bird in the wilderness,
> like a young owl haunting the wilderness. I lie awake and moan.
> I am like a solitary bird on the rooftop. (*Psalm 102:6-7*)

> God gives the animals their food,
> and the young ravens when they cry. (*Psalm 147:9*)

The psalmist marvels at the beauty of nature. Jesus senses a mysterious Presence and is drawn to praise:

I will extol you, my God and King,
 and bless you forever and ever.
Great is Yahweh, and greatly to be praised;
 his greatness is unsearchable.
One generation shall laud your works to another,
 and shall declare your mighty deeds.
I will meditate on the glorious splendour of your majesty,
 and on your wondrous works.
All your works shall give thanks to you, Yahweh,
 and all your faithful shall bless you.
They shall speak of the glory of your kingdom,
 and tell of your power.
The eyes of all look to you,
 and you give them their food in due season.
You open your hand, satisfying the desire of every living thing.
My mouth will speak the praise of Yahweh,
 and all flesh will bless you forever and ever. (*Psalm 145*)

When he sat with members of his extended family in the courtyard after a hard day's work, music lifted Jesus' heart to God:

It is good to give thanks to Yahweh, to sing praises to you;
to declare your steadfast love in the morning,
 and your faithfulness by night,
to the music of the lute and the harp, to the melody of the lyre.
For you, Yahweh, have made me glad by your work;
 at the works of your hands I sing for joy. (*Psalm 92:1-3*)

Rivers clap your hands; hills ring out your joy. (*Psalm 98:8*)

3. Jesus' baptismal experience

Jesus was in his early thirties when he heard that there was a prophet inviting people to undergo a complete purification in preparation for an encounter with the longed-for Messiah. Jesus joined the crowd who were being baptised in the Jordan by John. After his baptism Jesus had an overwhelming experience of being loved. He believed that it was God who was loving him. He related to this mysterious, gracious, presence as to a 'Father', and he identified as God's 'Son'.

As a young man, Jesus must have struggled with aspects of the God presented to him in the Scriptures and in the synagogue: a God who was so tender, but also so harsh. After his baptism, he felt immersed in a love that was unconditional. It refreshed his mind and heart. He knew that he had to escape to the desert to discover what this experience meant for him. In the desert, he came to see that God was calling him to go back to Galilee to show people that God wants us to know God as Jesus knows God, to know that we are unconditionally loved wherever we have strayed and whatever we have done. Jesus felt that God was calling him to show this by how he relates to us.

To enjoy the life God wants for us we have to make changes in our lives. Jesus called us to repent (Mark 1:15). However, it was clear to Jesus that God is not withholding love till we change. On the contrary, God is loving us as we are, and it is this love that makes change possible for us. This is the 'good news' that Jesus calls us to believe (Mark 1:16).

When Jesus returned to Nazareth, there was a new fire burning in his heart, and a new urgency. He had to leave everything to go wherever God's call took him. The love of God was burning in his heart, and he wanted to embrace everyone with the love that kept filling his heart. At his baptism, Jesus saw that God found him loveable: 'You are my Son. I delight in you'. Jesus believed that God was calling him to see that everyone is loveable.

We don't always see this. We need someone to believe in us. This is Jesus' mission. He saw how loveable people are, and he called on others to join him in seeing this. Central to love is respect – from the Latin *respicere* – meaning to take a second look. To love is to respect, to go deeper than a superficial glance. It is in this second look that we see that people are loveable. Jesus' manner with people, and his message of a God who loves, brought peace to people suffering from illnesses, including mental ones. People found a new meaning in their life. Crowds gathered to hear him speak and to feel his healing touch. People in their hundreds found new purpose and a new freedom. Jesus' love enabled people to believe what Jesus saw in them, what God revealed to them through Jesus about themselves, about others and about God.

4. Jesus' concept of God revealed in his teaching and actions

Jesus was born towards the end of the reign of Herod. Herod's son, Antipas, inherited the territory of Galilee. He set out to rebuild Sepphoris. Jesus' father, Joseph, was a builder. He, and perhaps one or other of his brothers, made their home in Nazareth, a small village, a short walk from Sepphoris. Antipas funded the rebuilding of Sepphoris with crippling taxes. Those, like Joseph and his son Jesus, who worked in the building trade were able to manage, but the same could not be said for most of the farmers who eked out a living on their small family holdings. To pay the taxes, they were forced to borrow, and when they failed to repay the loan, they forfeited their land. They were reduced to hiring themselves out as day labourers.

When they couldn't find employment, they had to beg to survive. Things got worse when Antipas set about building a new city bordering the lake. He called it Tiberias, after the Roman Emperor. The hopelessness of their situation led many small farmers to despair and depression.

On almost every page of the Gospels, we hear Jesus speaking of 'the kingdom of God': what the world would be like if we welcomed God's grace.

Jesus pictures God as a farmer who never gives up but keeps sowing good seed (*Matthew 13:3-32*). He pictures God as a shepherd who is willing to risk everything to search for a strayed sheep and bring it safely home (*Luke 15:3-7*). He pictures God as a woman who supplies enough yeast to feed whoever is hungry (*Matthew 13:13*).

God wants everyone to 'live to the full' (*John 10:10*). He welcomes everyone to a love banquet (*John 6:1-14*), including an inspiration for people to go out to let everyone know of the feast God is offering and to help everyone to respond to the invitation (*Matthew 22:1-10*).

By everyone the Gospel writer means all people, including a woman committing adultery (*see John's Gospel Chapter 8*). Jesus knows it is a sin, but to everyone's amazement he refuses to condemn her. He knows that we will help her change her behaviour by loving her, not condemning her (*John 8:3-11*).

God is constantly offering each of us the grace to love our neighbours whoever they are and whatever their circumstance. Jesus uses the image of a Samaritan being moved with compassion for a man molested by brigands (*Luke 10:29-37*). The Samaritan is an image of God's compassion. Jesus is inviting each of us to be an instrument of God's compassion to others.

Nowhere in Jesus' teaching is God's love more powerfully expressed than in Jesus' picture of a father's love for his two very different sons (*Luke 15:11-32*). The father longs for the younger son to come home, and when he returns the father does not reprimand him. He organises a feast and invites the whole town to come and celebrate his son's return.

When the older son is angry, the father leaves the party and comes out to him. The older son complains: 'Look! All these years I've been slaving for you and never disobeyed your orders. Yet you never gave me even a young goat so I could celebrate with my friends. But when this son of yours who has squandered your property with prostitutes comes home, you kill the fattened calf for him!' The father reminds his son: 'Son, you are always with me, and all that is mine is yours. We had to celebrate and rejoice, because your brother was dead and has come to life; he was lost and has been found' (*Luke 15:31-32*). He pleads with the older son to come in to share the celebration.

Jesus' image of God is clear from his teaching. His teaching is convincingly demonstrated in his actions. A leper came to him asking to be healed. Everyone, including the leper, thought that leprosy was a divine punishment for sin. To everyone's astonishment, Jesus embraces the leper and tells him to go and show those responsible that he is cured. He can re-join the community (*Mark 1:40-45*). A man paralysed by sin is brought to Jesus who shows God's love for him by healing not punishing him (*Mark 2:1-12*).

Pharisees see their role as enforcing what they see as God's will by insisting that sinners be avoided. They are shocked that Jesus eats with sinners. Jesus knows that God is Love and that the way to help people to cease sinning is to love them, not avoid or ostracise them (*Mark 2:15-17*).

People are afraid of those who are mentally disturbed. They think of them as inhabited by a demon, an unclean spirit. One of them is living among the tombs. No one can control him. Then he sees Jesus and something about Jesus attracts him, he gives in to the attraction. Jesus welcomes him and he finds peace (*Mark 5:1-20*).

Wherever Jesus went, people 'rushed about and began to bring the sick on mats to wherever they heard he was. And wherever he went, into villages or cities or farms, they laid the sick in the marketplaces, and begged him that they might touch even the fringe of his cloak; and all who touched it were healed' (*Mark 6:55-56*). Love is a wonderful healer. We should not be surprised that Jesus' love, when welcomed in faith, had such amazing effects.

It is clear from the Gospels that Jesus' desire was to do what he discerned to be the will of his Father. In the light of his baptismal experience and his experience of intimate communion with God, the gracious mystery, we would perhaps better express it as Jesus discerning what Love was inviting him to do. At first, he thought that God wanted him and his disciples to restrict his mission to Jews (*Matthew 10:5-6*). Then he met a Gentile woman from the region of Tyre. Her persistence in believing that Jesus could heal her daughter led Jesus to discern that it was God's will for him to respond to faith wherever he saw it (*Mark 7:24-30*).

More than anything else, it was their witnessing of Jesus' prayer that led those close to Jesus to realise that his compassionate love had its source in his communion with God (*Mark 1:35-38; 9:1-8*).

Jesus' heart reached out to everyone, and in so doing revealed God's love: 'Come to me, all you that are weary and are carrying heavy burdens, and I will give you rest. Take my yoke upon you and learn from me; for I am gentle and humble in heart, and you will find rest for your souls. For my yoke is easy, and my burden is light' (*Matthew 11:28-30*). He was speaking for God.

Jesus wants us to share his faith, his belief in God. In what may be Paul's earliest letter, and if so the earliest writing of the New Testament, composed only 15 years after Jesus' death, Paul writes: 'It is no longer I who live, it is Christ, the Messiah, who lives in me. The life I now live, I live by the faith of Jesus, who is loving me, giving himself for me' (*Galatians 2:20*). We are all called to make these words our own.

5. Jesus' God is full of compassion

From the Gospel record, it is clear that Jesus shares the faith of the people that God is compassionate (*see page 19*) and wants people to be free from anything that hinders them from 'living to the full' (*John 10:10*).

From his intimate communion with God, Jesus knows that his people are, indeed, God's 'treasured possession' (*see page 22*). It is clear from his ministry that Jesus believes that God has a special relationship with every people, with every person.

6. Jesus' God does not have enemies

Jesus challenges his disciples to be discerning when they read their sacred texts: 'Go and learn the meaning of the words' (*Matthew 9:13*). 'It was said to you of old, but I say to you' (*Matthew 5:42-43*). He does not portray God as a warrior conquering enemies (*see page 23*), He wants his disciples to love their enemies, and the reason he gives is that God loves them (*Matthew 5:44-48*). As we will now see, at the heart of Jesus' mission is the conviction that love is being poured into our universe, and it is for everyone.

7. Jesus' God is not a controlling, intervening, God

The sacred writings of Israel portray God as an intervening God (*see page 24*). The heart of Jesus' teaching, and the key to his mission, was his understanding of God. Jesus did not think of God as distant from creation, intervening whenever God wanted to see his will being done. He believed God to be constantly present everywhere and to everyone. Jesus told anyone who was willing to listen that they were to change and become like little children. He told them that God was their 'Father' and was not reacting to them to bless or to punish.

With God there is only blessing. We can't expect to avoid the consequences of the decisions we make, but God is the inspiring initiator who embraces us all, surrounding each of us with love and filling our minds and hearts. Jesus told people this and encouraged them to believe it by the way he opened his heart and his arms to everyone.

Jesus was fully involved in people's lives, but he regularly went off on his own. He wanted, he needed, to be alone with God. He needed to experience the intimacy which he experienced at his baptism. Communion with God was at the heart of his life, and he kept telling us that it had to be at the heart of our lives as well. It was Jesus' gift to tell everyone that God is love and to show how wonderful this is by how he, Jesus, responded to this love and invited all to share his response.

Jesus thought of God and responded to God in a personal way. He addressed God as 'Abba'. He invited us to do the same. Jesus believed that he could relate to God in a personal way. If we choose to believe Jesus, we, too, can relate to God in a personal way. However, we must take great care as to how we do this. We should not imagine God as being outside us, listening to us and responding. God is not intervening in our lives, either by taking the initiative or by responding to us. God is constantly present, creating, sustaining and inspiring us.

Some think that the crucifixion could not have happened if God did not will it. When we ask why Judas betrayed Jesus, why the high priest and Pilate behaved as they did, we should conclude that they were acting, not as instruments of God's will, but as Jesus said: 'You look for an opportunity to kill me, because there is no place in you for my word' (*John 8:37*).

Those responsible for crucifying Jesus were acting not as instruments of God's will but because they were resisting God's grace. God was present on Calvary not willing the innocent Jesus to be killed, but lovingly sustaining Jesus and loving people though him. God as revealed by Jesus is present wherever there is love.

God is all-powerful – all-powerful love! God does not override or control the exercise of human freedom, or the consequences of bad decisions. Jesus shows that our sinful behaviour cannot stop God loving.

It is critically important that we question how we picture God as intervening in our lives. God is not intervening, because God is always present surrounding us with love. The air we breathe is there all the time. It is not intervening. The sea in which a fish swims is there surrounding the fish. It is not intervening. Should we not picture God as a constant, sustaining, unchanging, loving presence?

When we cry out to God, hoping that our prayer will be heard and responded to, should we not rather picture God as constantly creating, sustaining, and graciously blessing us? We pray to God in order to focus our attention on the always loving, always blessing God. Focused in this way, we are open to believe, open to welcome grace.

Jesus invites us to be like children. We can petition God for anything we want, so long as we conclude our prayer as Jesus concluded his in Gethsemane: 'Father, not what I want, but what you want' (*Matthew 26:39*). (We will take a close look at Gethsemane in the next section). We are to pray to discern how best to open ourselves to the unchanging gracious God, our loving Father.

To picture God as intervening lands us in serious theological problems. If we understand God as intervening, we may well ask why God doesn't intervene to end violence or to feed starving people. It is not surprising that people doubt that such an apparently arbitrary God exists. Atheism feeds off such doubts. Is it not a more satisfactory view to recognise that the problem lies in our thinking that God intervenes?

God is not somewhere outside us who intervenes and then returns outside. Jesus invites us to believe in a God who is constantly present, constantly creating, sustaining, inspiring, constantly gracing. It is up to us to open our minds and hearts to commune with God and to welcome God's life-giving love. God's love does not protect us *from* all suffering. But it protects us *in* all suffering.

We humans are free to open our lives to God's loving or to ignore or reject it. Our choice has consequences. Instead of attributing to God the often-random developments in our emerging universe, should we not open our hearts to the ever-present God and find inspiration to make an intelligent contribution to the development of our world?

The purpose of prayer is not to get God to change in response to our petition. We pray in order to focus ourselves in such a way that we are open to the love that God is offering us. God did not intervene to free Jesus from the power of those who crucified him. Jesus believed that God never stopped loving him. Jesus kept believing in his Father's presence and sustaining grace. Because he yielded to this grace, he entrusted his life to God, confident that God's love would embrace him even on the cross and draw him into a communion of love beyond death.

Prayer is like a flower that opens its petals to the sun and rain. The sun of God's warmth and care is constant. The nurturing and refreshing rain of God's love is ever present. In prayer, we attend to God from within the situation in which we find ourselves. In our turning to God, we focus our attention, and we express our openness to receive whatever grace God is offering us – grace that, if we were not attending, we would fail to notice, fail to welcome.

God is the constant Self-Giver. God is love. To pray is to open ourselves to welcome God's Self-gift. We must look carefully at how we imagine God working what we are accustomed to call miracles. Some go so far as to think of miracles as proving that God exists because only God could act in such a miraculous way. Does not this way of thinking see God as a distinct being, rather than as a Presence who is at the heart of everything we experience? God is always creating, always giving God's Self in love.

We are free not to open ourselves to God's Self-gift and when we remain closed, we deprive ourselves of the gift and its consequences. Jesus invites us: 'Believe in God and believe in me' (John 14:1). When we use the word 'believe', it is important to know that 'lieve' is an Old English spelling of 'love'. To 'believe' is to choose to place ourselves in love, in God's love.

As I write this (2023), Turkey and Syria are suffering the consequences of massive earthquakes. Millions have been displaced. Thousands have lost their lives. Thanks to the heroic risk undertaken by so many people, hundreds of people have been rescued from the rubble. We ask: 'Where is God in all this?' Some see God as miraculously intervening to save those rescued. This leaves us with the question: why did God not intervene to save everyone? To ask why the earthquakes happened, we must turn to science. There is an explanation, too, for why some survived. To know where God is in a situation, we must look to see where love is. God is present inspiring the rescuers. God is present inspiring many nations to pour resources into caring for the displaced.

Those who turn to God in a disaster such as this are opening their minds and hearts to be inspired by the ever-present love of God to sustain their faith, to inspire their hope and to call on their love. When we look at the disaster of the Turkey-Syria earthquakes, we are amazed at the amount of love we see there. Jesus encourages us to trust that the thousands who were not rescued will, like Jesus, be welcomed by Love into God's eternal embrace.

Jesus was personally convinced of this (*see Matthew 22:31-32; John 11:25-26*). That there is a life that is beyond the life we now experience is central to the teaching of the Gospels and the Letters of the New Testament (*see 1 Corinthians 15*). This conviction is not meant to distract us to try to escape from living in the present moment by focusing on 'heaven'. It is meant to keep opening us to receive and give love in the real situation in which we find ourselves, however painful.

8. Jesus' dying

Jesus kept on meeting resistance, especially from those whose power he threatened. Some of the Pharisees resented Jesus' popularity. He stressed the need for compassion rather than submission to their interpretation of the Law. This covered even the law of the Sabbath which they rightly saw as being so central to fidelity to the covenant (*Mark 2:23-28*). Some of the greedy landowners resented Jesus' teaching on justice. Antipas had John killed. If Jesus was not so popular, Antipas would not have hesitated to have Jesus killed as well (*see Luke 13:31*).

In Judea, Jesus was far more vulnerable. Jerusalem was the centre of the priestly aristocracy and those responsible for the temple cult. Moreover, unlike Galilee, Judea was ruled directly by a military prefect appointed by Rome. The Jewish authorities were determined to nip in the bud any movement that might displease the Roman occupiers. On one of Jesus' rare visits to Jerusalem, he dared to challenge them. They determined to get rid of him before his Galilean followers arrived to celebrate the Passover. They captured Jesus and handed him over to Pilate, the Roman Prefect, with a trumped-up charge that Jesus was claiming to be the king of the Jews, which would make him a threat to Rome. Pilate agreed to have him crucified.

It was a time of great excitement. Pilgrims were flocking to Jerusalem to celebrate the Festival of Passover on that special Friday evening (*John 19:31*). Sensing that the end was nigh, and anticipating the feast, Jesus gathered the twelve (*Mark 14:17; Matthew 26:20. Luke 22:14* speaks of 'apostles') for what was to prove a final meal. He had promised them: 'where two or three are gathered in my name, I am there among them' (*Matthew 18:20*).

This was especially true of this last supper. He took the bread, broke it, and shared it with his disciples. His body was about to be broken. The breaking was done by sinful people. Jesus made this breaking – as he made everything – a gift of love. He took the poured-out wine. It was his lifeblood poured out for them, indeed for the world. Every time they gathered as his disciples, he promised to be with them, nourishing them, giving himself for them as he had always done.

After the supper, he went with his disciples to Gethsemane (*John 18:1*). He knew that the Jewish leaders had long been wanting to kill him. There was every possibility that they would act before the Galilean pilgrims arrived for the festival. He needed the support of his disciples, especially Peter, James and John, but when the horror of the situation crowded in on him and them, his disciples could not cope. Jesus was utterly alone, 'distressed and agitated. I am deeply grieved even to death' (*Mark 14:33-34*).

The thought of undergoing the dreadful death of crucifixion filled him with dread. As a boy of eight or nine, he had witnessed the defeat of the uprising led by Judas the Galilean. Hundreds of men were crucified, their crosses stretching from the hill country near Nazareth down to the plain.

A deeper source of bewilderment and pain may have been the thought that he had failed the mission given him by God. The Romans still occupied the Holy Land. The religious leaders, on the whole, persisted in closing their hearts to love. While many of the ordinary people had welcomed Jesus and his message of love, there were still lepers that needed to be welcomed, sinners who needed to hear of God's forgiveness, people broken by poverty who needed to be embraced by a community committed to care for them. And Jesus' closest disciples were obviously not ready to carry on his mission. Jesus cried out to his Father to give him more time to love, more time to reveal his Father's love.

As he prayed in the olive garden, a prayer arose from the depths of his being. He had always known the will of God present to him, present to the whole world. He had always known the will of God.

It was to love, to open our heart and our arms to love, no matter what. Jesus stood up from his prayer, strengthened by the belief that he was loved by God, and that God wanted to love people through him. Whatever his fears, whatever others might do to him, he knew what to do: 'not my will but yours be done' (*Mark 14:36*). Nothing would distract him from loving.

Tragically, betrayed by Judas, one of the twelve, Jesus was taken by the temple police, badly treated, and handed over to Pilate, who saw that it was to his advantage to give in to the wishes of the Jewish leaders, and add Jesus to the list of those to be crucified that day. According to Mark, Jesus was crucified mid-morning and died mid-afternoon. Mark gives us only one word spoken by Jesus from the cross. It is the opening words of Psalm 22: 'My God, my God, why have you forsaken me" (in Aramaic, 'Eloi, Eloi, lema sabachthani'). At one level, Mark is inviting us to reflect on the psalm as we contemplate the crucified Jesus. Psalm 22 begins in deep darkness but goes on to radiate the light of trust and communion.

Mark's text goes on to say that those witnessing the crucifixion understood Jesus to be calling 'Elijah come' (*Mark 15:35*). The same cry could be translated: 'My God, You!', which is found in Psalm 22 verse 10. This may be why Mark places the first words of Psalm 22 on Jesus' lips.

Matthew follows Mark. Luke invites us to reflect on other aspects of Jesus giving himself to us from the cross. He has Jesus say: 'Father, forgive them for they do not know what they are doing' (*Luke 23:34*). We cannot pretend away the consequences of our actions, but the Gracious Mystery we call 'God' does not cease loving when we sin. When one of the men being crucified with him sensed something special in Jesus, he asked: 'Jesus, remember me when you come into your kingdom'. Luke has Jesus respond: 'Truly, I tell you, today you will be with me in Paradise' (*Luke 23:43*). In the terrible agony of Calvary, Jesus knows that God is loving him – and whoever opens their hearts to God and believes. Luke concludes his account of Calvary: 'Jesus, crying with a loud voice, said, "Father, into your hands I commend my spirit". Having said this, he breathed his last' (*Luke 23:46*).

John reflects on the significance of Jesus' lifegiving on Calvary in the Supper Discourses (*John 14-17*). In his account of Jesus' dying he writes: "When Jesus saw his mother and the disciple whom he loved standing beside her, he said to his mother, "Woman, here is your son". Then he said to the disciple, "Here is your mother" (*John 19:26-27*). Those who were determined to destroy Jesus and to wipe away his memory, could not stop his gentle caring, revealing God's love. John adds two final words. He has Jesus say: 'I am thirsty' (*John 19:28*). Thirsty for communion with his Father, and for our love. Jesus' final words as presented by John are: 'It is accomplished' (*John 19:30*). The doubts that troubled him in Gethsemane are gone. 'Then he bowed his head and gave up his spirit' (*John 19:30*). He entrusted his last breath to God, and breathed his Spirit over the universe.

Part Five
Divine love in a human heart

1. What Jesus revealed continued after his death

The way Jesus related to people, and the way he spoke about God, was so profound that his dying did not lead to his being forgotten. He had shown them something they could not forget. This was especially true when the pilgrims came back from Jerusalem and told the people how Jesus died. Then came the news that some of Jesus' close followers had experiences that convinced them that, despite his being crucified and buried, Jesus was alive in the mystery of the communion with God that he had spoken about when he was with them (*See especially Luke and John's post-crucifixion accounts, and the Supper Discourses in John's Gospel*). How could Jesus' disciples forget the intimacy of love that Jesus had shown them, and the conviction that God was calling them to live to the full in a freedom they had never previously thought possible?

It is clear from the writings of the New Testament that Jesus' disciples were attracted by the beautiful humanity of Jesus. They grew to see that at the heart of his beautiful humanity was his intimate communion with God, his divinity. As Christianity spread through the Greek world, it became important to find words that expressed his divinity, while respecting his humanity and faithfully preserving monotheism. This proved to be a difficult task.

Constantine wanted Christianity to be an instrument in holding the Empire together. He summoned Church leaders to meet and sort out their differences. In 325 AD, they gathered at Nicaea, not far from Constantinople. Out of that council came the creed that we know as the Nicene Creed. It spoke of the Trinity: there is one God, but three persons In God. It spoke also of the

Incarnation: one of the persons of the Trinity, the Word, became a human being, Jesus.

The theologians of the day were doing what theologians have to do as one generation passes to another. They were approaching the mystery of Jesus greatly influenced by Platonic philosophy. The unity achieved in regard to the Trinity and the Incarnation was fragile. For hundreds of years, bishops, whole Christian communities, continued to disagree on how best to understand the relationship between Jesus and God. They struggled to find words that spoke of Jesus' humanity and divinity. Some highlighted Jesus' divinity, but in a way that denied the reality of Jesus' humanity. Others stressed Jesus' humanity, but in a way that denied his divinity.

We have a lot to learn about Jesus and so about God from the theology that developed in the early Church and is expressed in the creeds of the early Councils. What I am hoping to stress in this book is that we have a lot to learn also from keeping our focus on the New Testament, on what the authors have to say about Jesus and so about the God Jesus experienced and revealed.

At the heart of Christian faith is the belief that Jesus – having died – is alive, in communion with God and offering to us his Spirit, his prayer, his divine communion, his heart, his love, his faith. Paul puts it this way: 'It is no longer I who live. It is the Messiah who lives in me. The life I now live I live by the faith of the Son of God, loving me, giving himself for me' (*Galatians 2:20*). As Christians, we are invited to believe that Jesus is living in a way that transcends the kind of life that we experience. We are encouraged to believe that after death we will enjoy the same transcendent life. We are invited to believe in the God that Jesus believed in, the God of the living' (*Mark 12:27*).

2. Jesus is God's perfect human word

God reveals God's Self in creation. Every creature participates in God's being and is a word of God to us. This is beautifully true of

Jesus. The pure and intimate way Jesus reveals God led his disciples to speak of Jesus as God's 'Son', an intimate relationship we are all invited to share. They welcomed Jesus' invitation to know God as his and our 'Father'. They experienced God's Spirit in the love God has for Jesus and for them. When Jesus spoke of the 'kingdom (reign) of God', he was speaking of the communion in love into which God wants to draw every creature.

Being human, Jesus could not know God as an *object* of experience, but he was conscious of himself as deeply loved. He called out to the Lover, to God, in agony and in ecstasy, and he responded to what he believed was a call from God to give himself to people in love. Jesus believed in God as the One who faithfully loves him, loves everyone and everything. He experienced the whole of creation as an expression of God's gift of God's Self. In other words, he experienced love and believed it was God who was loving him and every created being.

It was obvious to those who knew Jesus that Jesus was human like them, but there was something quite special about him: his extraordinary healing and liberating love. They came to see that this amazing love came from his special communion with God whom he called 'Abba'. Knowing God as Father, Jesus knew himself as God's 'Son'.

Jesus' experience of intimate communion with the mysterious Presence we call God led him to believe that God is Love. Moreover, he invited us to open our minds and hearts to welcome God's gift of God's Self to us in love, and to allow this divine love to flow through us to others, indeed to the whole universe. If we seek God, if we want to know where to find God, Jesus' teaching and his way of relating encourage us to believe that when we experience love, when we experience one being going beyond what it is by giving itself to another, we are experiencing God.

When Jesus speaks of God, he is speaking from his experience of being loved unconditionally. He believed that God was the source of this love. The Beloved Disciple expresses this beautifully in the Prologue to his Gospel: 'No one has ever seen God. It is the only Son, who is in the bosom of the Father, who has made God known' (*John 1:18*). The Beloved Disciple has Jesus put it this way: 'The Father knows me, and I know the Father ... The Father loves me' (*John 10:15,17*). This is a special use of the word 'know', a usage found throughout the Bible. In one of the creation stories we read: 'The man knew his wife Eve and she conceived and bore Cain' (*Genesis 4:1*). There is no contradiction with what we wrote earlier when distinguishing knowing and believing (*see page 7*). It is a special use of the word knowing to speaks of an intimate love-communion.

When the New Testament speaks of the Spirit, it is speaking of the intimate giving and receiving of love flowing between Jesus and God. Those who experienced Jesus came to see him as God's perfect human Word, God's perfect human Self-revelation. As Matthew writes: 'They will call him Immanuel, a name which means God-is-with-us' (*Matthew 1:23*). The role of Jesus extends beyond his example and teaching. The faith of the Christian community has always included the conviction that Jesus is alive and active in our world. We are invited to welcome Jesus' personal love and to respond in love. This belief helps keep our focus on God as love. It also challenges us to grow beyond where we are by giving ourselves to others in love.

In examining who Jesus is, it is essential that we keep our focus on him. The danger of beginning our search by focusing on the credal statements that came out of the early Greek Councils is that, instead of coming to know Jesus the way his early disciples came to know him, we will be beginning our search by focusing on the necessarily mysterious God. Inevitably, we will think of Jesus as a divine person with a human mind and heart and body. We will find ourselves thinking of his humanity existing in time, and his person as being eternal. We will find ourselves denying that he is 'like us in everything except sin'.

The New Testament uses the word 'God' nearly twelve hundred times. The reference is to the One Jesus believed in, prayed to, and spoke of, the God he called by the affectionate word 'Abba, the God Jesus revealed in all he was, in all he said and did. In the man Jesus God is manifesting God's presence.

When, before knowing Jesus, the disciples had sought an answer to the question 'Who is God?', they had looked to the Exodus event and seen God revealed as a liberator and saviour, as the God of faithful, covenant love. Now, having come to know Jesus, and having experienced a new covenant of love and a new liberation and fullness of life, they looked to Jesus to reveal God. They came to believe that 'in the Messiah God was reconciling the world to God' (*2 Corinthians 5:19*).

To answer the question 'Who is God?', Jesus' disciples learned to contemplate Jesus. To answer the question 'Who is Jesus?', they learned to look upon him as the presence and revelation of the God in whom he and they believed. They saw this in everything Jesus was, in everything he did and said. It was especially seen on the cross: 'When you have lifted up the Son of Man, then you will know that I am' (*John 8:28*). 'I am' translates the Greek *ego eimi*, which translates a Hebrew expression, *ehyeh*, that is linked to Yahweh, the 'name' revealed to Moses at the burning bush (*Exodus 3:14, see page 11*). Jesus revealed the One he addressed as Father ('Abba), as the redeemer God. It was from the pierced heart of Jesus on the cross that Jesus' disciples experienced the power of Jesus' life-giving Spirit in their lives.

Matthew captures something of this in his final portrait in which he presents the exalted Jesus in glory on a mountain in Galilee. The Risen Jesus authoritatively commissions his disciples to carry on his mission of bringing about the reign of God. He promises them in words that speak of the presence and power of God: 'Know that I am with you always; yes, to the end of the age' (*Matthew 28:20*).

3. Jesus is God with us

The first Christians were Jews, and monotheists. Saul of Tarsus, better known to us by his Roman name Paul, is the clearest example we have of Jews who looked on Christians as blasphemously worshipping Jesus. Paul had a series of experiences that radically changed his understanding of Christianity. His letters, the earliest of which is only fifteen or so years after Jesus' death, demonstrate that the special place of Jesus in Christian life dates from the very beginnings of the Jesus movement. They demonstrate also that the unique place of Jesus in Christian understanding in no way lessens Christian commitment to monotheism.

The Christian community embraced the practice of keeping Jesus in focus when they spoke of 'God'. As Paul acclaims: Jesus is 'the image of the unseen God' (*Colossians 1:15*). We find this in John's Gospel, composed in the last decade of the first century. In response to Philip's desire to see God, Jesus says: 'To have seen me is to have seen the Father ... Do you not believe that I am in the Father, and the Father is in me?' (*John 14:8-10*). We find it also in a letter written by Ignatius, bishop of Antioch, in the opening years of the second century. In a letter to the Christian community in Ephesus Ignatius wrote: 'Our God, even Jesus the Messiah, was borne in the womb by Mary according to the dispensation of God, of the seed of David and of the Holy Spirit' (*Ephesians, 18*).

In his letter to the Christian community in Rome, Ignatius wrote: 'Suffer me to copy the passion of my God' (*Romans, 6*). It is possible that an example of this practice of focusing on Jesus while speaking of God is found in the Prologue to John's Gospel. Some early manuscripts read: 'No one has ever seen God. It is the only Son, who is in the bosom of the Father, who has made God known' (John 1:18). Other manuscripts add the word '***God***': "No one has ever seen God. It is ***God*** the only Son, who is in the bosom of the Father, who has made God known' (*John 1:18*).

When Christians worshipped God, they included Jesus, of course in a way that is consistent with strict monotheism. What set the Christian use of the word 'God' apart from its use by every other group was that Jesus' disciples believed that to speak of God we have learned to keep our eyes on Jesus. For them, it is Jesus who reveals the one true God. It is Jesus who is God's Word to us. It is not that Christians worshipped God and in a parallel way worshipped Jesus. Christians were strict monotheists. Worship was offered to God, and only to God. They insisted that the God they worshipped is the God seen in and revealed by Jesus.

The practice of focusing on Jesus when speaking of God also witnesses to the fact that they were not content to admire Jesus while failing to listen to or watch God being revealed in and through him. The essence of Christianity is that in listening to Jesus, in watching him, and in experiencing something of the intimacy of his prayer, and welcoming a share in his faith, we are truly being drawn into communion with God.

Christianity quickly spread into the Roman polytheistic world. We have a letter written to the emperor Trajan early in the second century by Pliny the Younger who was a special imperial legate in Bithynia. He wrote that Christians 'chant antiphonally a hymn to Christ as to a god'. It is understandable that a man who was part of the Roman polytheistic world would interpret Christian behaviour in this way, but is this a true picture of Christian worship?

When we Christians speak of Jesus as 'God', we are not claiming that Jesus is *another* God. Jesus is a man, but in such an extraordinary purity that it is God, the one God in whom Jews and Christians believe, who is revealed in and through him. As we noted earlier, God is revealed in and through everything. This is true nowhere more beautifully than in Jesus of Nazareth. That is Christian belief. That is how Christians understand their experience.

Christians came to speak of Jesus as having two natures. The word 'nature' is a scientific term born of observation. We come to know something's nature by observing what it does. When his disciples watched Jesus and listened to him, his human nature was obvious. He showed them what we human beings can be at our best.

But they came to see more than this. They came to believe that what Jesus was saying and doing was revealing God, insofar as God can be revealed in a human being. That is Jesus' divine nature.

Jesus' followers were amazed at the purity and beauty of Jesus' love. Through Jesus' teaching and actions, they came to believe that God, the one God who is the source of all and who holds everything and everyone in existence, is Self-bestowing Love. They believed that the human Jesus was totally caught up in this divine love. It is God who heals through Jesus. It is God who loves through him. Jesus and the God he called 'Father' are one in a complete communion. It is their mutual love that is spoken of as the 'Holy Spirit'. Jesus believed that it was God's will that he share this Spirit of love with his disciples, and ultimately with every person on earth.

In his Second Letter, Peter prays that his readers 'may share in the divine nature' (*2 Peter 1:4*). Jesus shared in the divine nature. He wants us to share the intimate communion that he has with God, so that we, too, will speak God's words, be instruments to each other of God's life-giving love, and so reveal God as Love.

It was largely their experience of sharing in this love that explains the growth of Christian communities, and that attracted people to find in the Christian community a way of life that satisfied their search for meaning. As Paul wrote in his Letter to the Christian community in Rome: 'Hope does not disappoint us, because God's love has been poured into our hearts through the Holy Spirit that has been given to us' (*Romans 5:5*). To the community in Philippi, he wrote: 'If there is any appeal in the Messiah, any consolation from love, any communion in the Spirit, any movements of compassion and feelings of love, make my joy complete: be of the same mind, having the same love, being of one soul and one mind ... Let the same mind be in you that was in the Messiah Jesus' (*Philippians 2:1-2, 5*).

4. The Trinity

My focus here is on the New Testament. The teaching of the early Church theologians and the early Church creeds on the Trinity is outside the scope of this book. The Gospels and Letters of the New Testament invite us to begin our understanding of Jesus where the disciples began – with his real and attractive humanity. As we come to know the human Jesus, we, like Jesus' first disciples, are drawn to contemplate his prayer, and so his divinity: his communion with God, their shared Spirit.

As we are about to see, the New Testament often speaks in trinitarian terms as God, Jesus, and the Spirit. Its language is simpler than the abstract Greek terms that we find in the early councils. In the New Testament, the word 'God', while referring to One who is necessarily mysterious, is essentially quite straight-forward. God refers to the One whom Jesus communed with in prayer, and whom Jesus related to as his 'Father'.

'Jesus', too, is quite straightforward. He is 'Jesus, son of Joseph from Galilee' (*John 1:45*), 'the carpenter's son' (*Matthew 13:55*). Jesus looked to God for everything he was. He identified as God's 'Son' (*See Jesus' baptism experience, page 35*). In the New Testament, he is frequently referred to as the 'Messiah' (the 'Christ'): his disciples looked to him as God's answer to the longing of his people for One whom their God promised would free them to live to the full. Jesus is frequently referred to as 'Lord': a title which links him intimately to Yahweh, the God of the burning bush. Christians did not want to speak of 'God' without insisting that people looked to Jesus, for it was he who revealed the true God in his person, in his teaching and activity.

The word 'Spirit' is necessarily many-faceted for it speaks of the inner life of God and of Jesus. As we will now see, in the New Testament Trinitarian texts, we are invited to see Spirit as referring to the intimate love that draws Jesus into prayer, a love he wants everyone to experience.

Before we reflect on trinitarian texts found in the writings of the New Testament, let us play with some images. You are in a foreign country and you want to enjoy the local dance. You will need the help of a dancer. You learn a lot by watching the dancer, but you will get to really know the dance only by letting yourself get caught up in the dancing. Imagine God as the dance. To see the dance, you will need to watch the dancer, you will need to watch Jesus. This is essential, but it is not enough. Jesus invites you to join him in the dancing, made possible by the Spirit that is poured into our hearts (*Romans 5:5*).

Another image. You want to know a local song. You will need to listen to a singer, and to join in the singing. Imagine God as the song. To hear the song, you will need to listen to the singer, you will need to listen to Jesus. This is essential, but it is not enough. Jesus invites you to join him in the singing, made possible by the Spirit that is poured into our hearts.

A third image. The community of the Beloved Disciple tell you that 'God is love' (*1 John 4:16*). You can't see God. To grasp what they are saying, you need to watch and learn from a lover, from Jesus who incarnates divine love in a human heart. You will need to respond to his invitation to join him in welcoming God's love. and you need to be caught up in his loving by sharing the Spirit that is poured into our hearts, a loving that flows to others.

Let us now read the trinitarian texts found in the New Testament. Note that in none of these texts does 'God' refer to either Jesus (in **bold**) or the Spirit (in *italics*). In the New Testament, the trinitarian formulas refer to God, the man Jesus of Nazareth, and the Spirit: the communion of love that flows from God to Jesus and from Jesus to God.

Let us look first at Paul's letters. Paul did not know Jesus before Jesus' death. Whatever he learned about Jesus' teaching and actions he learned from Jesus' disciples. Paul does claim to experiencing an intimate communion with the Risen Jesus. It is this intimate communion that permeates his writing.

We begin with his Letter to the Galatians, perhaps his first extant letter composed only fifteen or so years after Jesus' death, and some seventeen years before the first of the Gospels.

"God has sent the *Spirit* of his **Son** into our hearts crying 'Abba! Father!" (*Galatians 4:6*).

It is God who pours into the heart of Jesus the divine Spirit of love-communion. Jesus knows that the life he experiences is given to him by God, and he responds by calling God his Father. Paul believes that God continues to embrace the Risen Jesus in love and wants to draw everyone to share Jesus' communion. God does this by 'sending the Spirit of his Son into our hearts' (Romans 5:5). The core of Christian life is the belief in the presence in the community and in our hearts of the Trinity: God, God's Son Jesus, and the Spirit of love that is their shared communion.

We find the same Trinitarian language in Paul's First Letter to the Thessalonians sent from Corinth in 50AD. Paul writes:

> Give thanks in all circumstances; for this is the will of God in the **Messiah Jesus** for you. Do not quench the Spirit (*1 Thessalonians 5:11-12*).

Paul is appealing to the Christian community in Thessalonica to give free rein to God's Spirit, the Spirit of love that binds the Messiah Jesus to God.

Paul uses trinitarian language in his follow-up letter to the Thessalonian community:

> We must always give thanks to God for you, beloved by the **Lord**, because God chose you to be holy by the *Spirit* (*2 Thessalonians 2:13*).

Holiness is the one word in the Bible that belongs only to God. When a person or a place is said to be holy, we are being told that God is present in that person or place. It is God's will to draw everyone into the holiness that God shares with Jesus through the gift of God's Spirit. The Thessalonian community is 'beloved by the Lord', is loved by Jesus who frees us from whatever is hindering us from living a full life of intimate communion with God. Paul invites us to be filled with gratitude for the gift of life given to us by Jesus.

We have two letters from Paul to the Christian community in Corinth.

> You were washed, you were sanctified, you were justified in the name of the **Lord Jesus, the Messiah**, and in the *Spirit* of our God (*1 Corinthians 6:11*).

The Risen Jesus, the promised Messiah, the Lord sent by God to liberate people from all that hinders our living to the full, is the One who cleanses us from sin, who draws us to share in God's holiness, who invites us into intimate relationship with God.

> There are varieties of gifts, but the same *Spirit*. There are varieties of ministries, but the same **Lord**. There are varieties of ways of exercising power, but it is the same God who activates all of them in everyone (*1 Corinthians 12:4-6*).

The Corinthian community can be likened to an orchestra. Each person in it has his or her unique gift. Paul assures them that each person's gift is a sharing in the Spirit of love that unites Jesus and God. He goes on to assure them that, while the gift is for them, it is also at the heart of their sharing in the liberating mission of Jesus, the Risen Lord. It is God who empowers their gift and their ministry, for it is a personal and communal expression of the power of God working in and through them.

> It is God who establishes us with you in the **Messiah**, and has anointed us, by putting his seal on us and giving us His *Spirit* (*2 Corinthians 1:21-22*).

> You are a letter of the **Messiah** ... written with the *Spirit* of the living God (*2 Corinthians 3:3*).

When Paul looks into the hearts of the Christian community in Corinth, he reads there a letter of love to him from the Risen Jesus. He wants the community to look into their own hearts. That is where they will find God and Jesus and the Spirit of love, a love they are invited to share.

> The grace of the Lord Jesus, the **Messiah**, the love of God, and the communion of the *Holy Spirit* be with all of you (*2 Corinthians 13:13*).

Paul spent the winter of 56-57AD in Corinth. It was there that he composed his Letter to the churches of Rome. He speaks of God, of Jesus, and of the Spirit that flows between them:

> You are in the *Spirit* since the *Spirit* of God dwells in you. Anyone who does not have the *Spirit* of the **Messiah** does not belong to him (*Romans 8:9*).

The Spirit is the bond of love filling the heart of God and the heart of the Messiah, Jesus.

> If the *Spirit* of God who raised **Jesus** from the dead dwells in you, He who raised the **Messiah** from the dead will give life to your mortal bodies also through His *Spirit* that dwells in you (*Romans 8:11*).

> When we cry 'Abba! Father!' it is the *Spirit* bearing witness that we are children of God, and if children, then heirs, heirs of God and joint heirs with the **Messiah** (*Romans 8:15-17*).

We find the same language in the circular letter composed perhaps during Paul's period of house-arrest in Caesarea.

> I pray that the God of our **Lord Jesus the Messiah**, the Father of glory, may give you a *Spirit* of wisdom and revelation as you come to know him (*Ephesians 1:17*).

> Through the **Messiah Jesus**, both of us [Jew and Gentile] have access in one *Spirit* to the Father (*Ephesians 2:18*).

The religion of Israel has its origin in the liberation from the slavery of Egypt, the journey through the wilderness and the settling in the land of Canaan. In the wilderness the people lived in tents. Trusting that God was with them, they constructed a tent for Yahweh, which they pitched outside the camp. When they settled in the land, they constructed a temple in which they believed God dwelt among them. In the Prologue to his Gospel, John asserts that in Jesus God's Word 'dwelt ('pitched his tent') among us' (*John 1:14*). God chose to dwell in Jesus, and in those who opened their hearts to welcome Jesus and his Spirit. Through the gift of his Spirit, each Christian and the Christian community became a temple in which God chooses to dwell.

> In the **Messiah Jesus** you also are built together into a dwelling place for God in the *Spirit* (*Ephesians 2:22*).

> There is one *Spirit* ... one **Lord** ... one God and Father of all (*Ephesians 4:4-6*).

In a letter written from house-arrest in Rome to the Christian community in Philippi, Paul, referring to the Risen Jesus, asserts that 'God gave him a name that is above every name', and at this name 'every knee should bend'. He goes on to proclaim that the name is 'Lord' (*Philippians 2:9-11*). At the burning bush, God is revealed to Moses as determined to redeem his people from the slavery of Egypt. This is expressed in the word 'Yahweh'. The practice grew of speaking the word 'Adonay', translated as 'Lord', where the text read 'Yahweh'. When the name 'Lord' is used of the Risen Jesus, it is a declaration that it is God's will to redeem his people through the person and ministry of Jesus.

In the same letter, Paul writes:

> We worship in the *Spirit* of God and boast in the **Messiah Jesus** (*Philippians 3:3*).

In his Letter to Titus, Paul writes:

> God our Saviour poured out the *Holy Spirit* on us richly through **Jesus, the Messiah, our Saviour** (*Titus 3:6*).

We find the same trinitarian language in other New Testament Letters.

> If you are reviled for the name of the **Messiah**, you are blessed, because the *Spirit* of glory, which is the *Spirit* of God, is resting on you (*1 Peter 4:14*).

There are those who have shared in the *Holy Spirit* and have tasted the goodness of the word of God but go on crucifying the **Son** of God (*Hebrews 6:4-6*).

The **Messiah** through the eternal *Spirit* offered himself to God (*Hebrews 9:14*).

By this you know the *Spirit* of God: every spirit that confesses that **Jesus the Messiah** has come in the flesh is from God (*1 Peter 4:2*).

Pray in the *Holy Spirit*. Keep yourselves in the love of God. Look forward to the mercy of our **Lord Jesus, the Messiah** (*Jude 20-21*).

We do what pleases God. And this is his commandment that we should believe in God's **Son Jesus, the Messiah**, and love one another just as he has commanded us. All who obey His commandments abide in him and he abides in them. By this we know that he abides in us, by the *Spirit* God has given us (*1 John 3:22-24*).

The Gospel of Matthew concludes with a reference to the Trinity: Having described Jesus' death and burial, Matthew concludes his Gospel with the Risen Jesus commissioning his disciples: 'Make disciples of all nations, baptising them in the name of the Father and of the Son and of the Holy Spiri' (Matthew 28:19). We reflected earlier on the importance to Jesus of his baptismal experience (*see page 35*). He wants everyone to share this experience: to know God's intimate love by opening our hearts to God's Spirit.

Throughout his Gospel, Luke invites us to contemplate the Trinity.

The *Holy Spirit* will come upon you, Mary, and the power of the Most High will overshadow you. Therefore, the child to be born will be holy. He will be called **Son** of God (*Luke 1:35*).

It had been revealed to Simeon by the *Holy Spirit* that he would not see death before he had seen the Lord's **Messiah** (*Luke 2:26*).

When Jesus had been baptised and was praying, the heaven was opened and the *Holy Spirit* descended upon him, and a voice came from heaven 'You are my **Son**, the Beloved, with you I am well pleased (*Luke 3:21-22 = Matthew 3:16-17 = Mark 1:10-11*).

These words are drawn from Isaiah 42. The Gospel-writers could find no better words to highlight Jesus' religious experience and mission.

Jesus rejoiced in the *Holy Spirit* and said: 'I thank you, Father, Lord of heaven and earth' (*Luke 10:21*).

Jesus said: If you know how to give good gifts to your children, how much more will the heavenly Father give the *Holy Spirit* to those who ask him (*Luke 11:13*).

In his Gospel, the Beloved Disciple invites us to enter the Heart of Jesus, and so to know as best we can the intimate love-communion of Jesus and God.

He whom God has sent speaks God's words, for he gives the *Spirit* without measure (*John 3:34*).

Jesus said: 'I am in the Father and the Father is in me ... If you love me, you will keep my commandments, and I will ask the Father, and he will give you another *Advocate* to be with you forever, the *Spirit* of truth ... He abides with you, and he will be in you. Those who love me will keep my word and my Father will love them and we will come to them and make our home with them' (*John 14:10, 15-17, 23*).

The Beloved Disciple knows that the Risen Jesus has chosen to make his home in the heart of each disciple. Where Jesus is, there is God, there is the Spirit of love that binds Jesus to God. Each disciple is invited to share the love communion in the heart of the Trinity.

The advocate, the *Holy Spirit*, whom the Father will send in **my** name, will teach you everything, and remind you of all that **I** have said to you (*John 14:26*).

> When the *Advocate* comes, whom **I** will send to you from the Father, the *Spirit* of truth who comes from the Father, he will testify on **my** behalf (*John 15:26-27*).

We go to the Acts of the Apostles to conclude our presentation of the trinitarian texts of the New Testament:

> Signs and wonders are performed in the name of your holy servant, **Jesus** ... They were all filled with the *Holy Spirit* and spoke the word of God with boldness (*Acts 4:30-31*).

> God exalted **Jesus** ... We are witnesses, and so is the *Holy Spirit* whom God has given to those who obey (*Acts 5:31-32*).

> Filled with the *Holy Spirit*, Stephen gazed into heaven and saw the glory of God and **Jesus** standing at the right hand of God (*Acts 7:55*).

> God anointed **Jesus** of Nazareth with the Holy Spirit (*Acts 10:38*).

> The *Holy Spirit* has made you overseers, to shepherd the church of God that God obtained by the blood of his own **Son** (*Acts 20:28*).

The constancy of these Trinitarian texts in the New Testament alerts us to the importance of keeping Jesus before our eyes when we think of the always present, mysterious God, and to keep listening to him, especially as Jesus draws us to enter our hearts and our community to discover there the Spirit of love that Jesus experiences and the communion he has with the Father, a communion that we are called to enjoy with him.

5. Misunderstanding the relationship of Jesus and God

In the two thousand years of Christianity, has there ever been a time free from misunderstanding the relationship between Jesus and God? The Gospel of the Beloved Disciple (the Gospel of John) witnesses to the fact that misunderstanding this relationship was already a factor in the debates of the last decade of the first century when the Gospel was composed. It is evident that Jews who accepted Jesus as the promised Messiah were debating with Jews who did not accept Jesus as the Messiah (the group called 'the Jews' in the Gospel).

The Beloved Disciple in his Gospel constantly focuses on Jesus' communion with God:

> The one who comes from heaven (from communion with God) testifies to what he has seen and heard (*John 3:31-32*).

> The one who is from God has 'seen' the Father (*John 6:46*).

Jesus experienced himself as on a mission given him by God (*see the reflections on Jesus' baptism, page 35*).

> The living Father has sent me, and I live because of the Father (*John 6:57*).

> I know the Father, because I am from the Father and it is the Father who sent me (*John 7:29*).

Jesus' words flow from his communion with God.

> He whom God has sent speaks God's words, for he gives the Spirit without measure (*John 3:34*).

> My teaching is not mine. It is from the Father who sent me. Anyone who resolves to do the will of God will know whether the teaching is from God or whether I am speaking on my own (*John 7:16-17*).

> I declare to the world what I have learned from God ... I speak these things as the Father instructed me (*John 8:26, 28*).

> I declare what I have seen in my Father's presence (*John 8:38*).

> I know God, and I keep God's word (*John 8:55*).

> Do you not believe that I am in the Father and the Father is in me? The words I say to you I do not speak as from myself (*John 14:10*).

> The word that you hear is not mine. It is from the Father who sent me (*John 14:24*).

In a prayer to God, Jesus says:

> The words that you gave me I have given to them, and they have received them and know in truth that I came from you; and they have believed that you sent me (*John 17:8*).

In John chapter 5, we find an account of Jesus healing a man on the Sabbath. We are told:

> The Jews started persecuting Jesus, because he was doing such things on the Sabbath (*John 5:16*).

We are then given Jesus' response:

> My Father is still working, and I also am working (*John 5:17*).

The text continues:

> For this reason, the Jews were seeking all the more to kill him, because he was not only breaking the Sabbath, but was also calling God his own Father, thereby making himself equal to God (*John 5:18*).

That this is not how the community of the Beloved Disciple understood Jesus' claim is clear from their account of Jesus' response:

> Jesus said to them: 'Very truly, I tell you, the Son can do nothing on his own, but only what he sees the Father doing; for whatever the Father does, the Son does likewise. The Father loves the Son and shows him all that the Father is doing' (*John 5:19-20*).

Jesus is not 'making himself equal to God'. His words come from his communion with God. So do his actions:

> My food is to do the will of the One who sent me and to complete God's work (*John 4:34*).

> The Son can do nothing on his own, but only what he sees the Father doing. For whatever the Father does, the Son does

likewise. The Father loves the Son and shows him all that the Father is doing (*John 5:19-20*).

I have come from heaven (from his intimate communion with God), not to do my own will, but the will of the One who sent me (*John 6:38*).

I can do nothing on my own. As I hear, I judge; and my judgment is just, because I seek to do not my own will but the will of the One who sent me (*John 5:30*).

The deeds that the Father has given me to complete, the very deeds that I am doing, testify on my behalf that the Father has sent me (*John 5:36*).

When you have lifted up the Son of Man, then you will realise that I AM, and that I do nothing on my own. The Father who sent me is with me and has not left me alone, for I always do what is pleasing to my Father (*John 8:28-29*).

The expression 'I AM' links Jesus' mission with that of Moses, sent by Yahweh to liberate people from slavery in Egypt (*see page 11; Exodus 3:14*).

It is the Father living in me who is doing this work (*John 14:10*).

Father, I glorified you on earth by finishing the work that you gave me to do (*John 17:4*).

Whoever believes in me believes not in me but in the One who sent me. And whoever sees me sees the One who sent me. I have come as light into the world, so that everyone who believes in me should not remain in the darkness (*John 12:44-46*).

It is from his intimate communion with God that Jesus experiences the call and the grace to share with others the revelation that he receives from God:

I do nothing on my own, but I speak these things as the Father instructed me. And the one who sent me is with me. The

Father has not left me alone, for I always do what is pleasing to my Father (*John 8:28-29*).

I declare to the world what I have heard from my Father (*John 8:26*).

I declare what I have seen in the Father's presence (*John 8:38*).

The author of the Letter to the Hebrews reminds us that Jesus 'had to become like his brothers and sisters in every respect' (Hebrews 2:17). He goes on the say: 'In every respect he has been tested as we are, yet without sin' (Hebrews 4:15).

When the authors of the New Testament say that Jesus did not sin, they are stating that Jesus never failed to welcome his Father's love and to obey his Father in everything he said and did.

In his Letter to the Christians in Philippi, Paul exhorts us:

Let the same mind be in you that was in Christ Jesus (*Philippians 2:5*).

He quotes an early Christian hymn that sings of Jesus being 'in the form (the human form) of God' (*Philippians 2:6*), echoing what God wants human beings to be in contrast with the sinful behaviour described in Genesis. Unlike Adam, 'Jesus did not regard equality with God as something to be grasped' (*Philippians 2:6*). Trusting in God, Jesus accepted the limitations of the human condition even when his fidelity to God meant he was crucified (*Philippians 2:7-8*).

Jesus did not, he could not, experience God as an object. He was conscious of himself as being loved, and, drawing on the tradition in which he was nurtured, he interpreted the experience as coming from the one he was brought up to call 'God'. When he declares that his whole desire was to do God's will, there was nothing blind or unthinking about his obedience. The word 'obedient' means listening (Latin *audiens*) and from close union (Latin *ob*). Jesus had to apply all his heart and soul and mind and strength to discern how best to respond to the love he experienced. He did this so beautifully and faithfully that his disciples attempted to follow his example and to live in the same Spirit. This is the essence of Christianity.

Jesus' disciples came to see him as the perfect human expression (the human embodiment, the 'incarnation') of God. When we speak of Jesus' divinity, we are speaking of his intimate communion with God:

> I am not alone; the Father is with me (*John 16:32*).

Such was the intimacy of this communion that Jesus could say: 'The Father and I are one' (*John 10:30*).

Here again, 'the Jews' misunderstood his claim: 'The Jews took up stones again to stone him. Jesus replied, "I have shown you many good works from the Father. For which of these are you going to stone me?"'

The Jews answered: 'It is not for a good work that we are going to stone you, but for blasphemy, because you, though only a human being, are making yourself God' (*John 10:31-33*).

Jesus was never 'making himself God'. Nor were his disciples. Jesus' claim, and the claim of Christians, is that Jesus is 'God's Son' (*John 10:36*). He enjoyed such intimate communion with God that he could say: 'The Father is in me, and I am in the Father' (*John 10:38*).

Jesus saw his mission as inviting us to share this communion. He likened himself to a vine. We are all graced to be branches, drawing life from him.

The Spirit of God filled his heart, his prayer, his life. Jesus revealed God in the love that flowed from this communion, a love, as already noted, that gave authority to his words, and healing and liberating power to his relationships. And Jesus wants us all to experience this communion.

> The Spirit abides in you and will be in you (*John 15:17*).

> You will know that I am in my Father, and you in me, and I in you (*John 14:20*).

> My Father will love you, and we will come to you and make our home with you (*John 14:23*).

Part Six
Sharing Jesus' faith

1. Jesus' faith

When Paul looks back on his behaviour prior to his enlightenment on the road to Damascus (*c. 34AD*), he knows that he was being driven by his ego. In his Letter to the Galatians, composed after his enlightenment, perhaps in 48 AD and, if so, his earliest extant letter, he writes: 'It is no longer I who live. It is the Messiah who lives in me. The life I now live in the flesh, I live by the faith of the Son of God, loving me, giving himself for me' (*Galatians 2:20*).

We catch faith from Jesus, our 'leader in faith' (*Hebrews 12:2*). As has been noted a number of times, being human, Jesus could not directly experience God, but he was conscious of himself as deeply loved, and he shared the way he conceived God as Love. The Gospels witness to this. As we saw earlier, it was Jesus' experience at his baptism that set the scene for his public ministry. The Gospels capture the essence of Jesus' religious experience by quoting God's words found in the Isaiah scroll: "You are my Son. I love you. I delight in you" (*Mark 1:11; see Isaiah 42:1*).

Jesus had an overwhelming experience of being loved and he believed it was by God. He went into the desert to struggle with what this experience might mean. He came to believe that God was calling him to reach out to people to show us that God wants us to have the same experience as Jesus had at his baptism. He wants us to know how much God loves us. As Jesus put it: 'I have come that you may live and live to the full' (*John 10:10*).

Impressed as they were by Jesus, his disciples grew to share Jesus' faith. Impressed by the quality of the lives lived by believers, people down through the centuries have been attracted to believe in the God Jesus believes in, and they have continued to believe because of the way this belief has enhanced their lives. This belief has been the contribution of the Christian community to the world.

God is constantly active in history, not intervening but constantly creating, constantly sustaining, constantly attracting everything in love. Jesus helps us to see and feel what this loving presence and action is like. He enables us to find words to direct us to better ways of thinking of God. He is a constant corrective to our tendency to misunderstand God by projecting onto God our limited concepts and dysfunctional habits of thinking.

The history of religion demonstrates how we project onto God our hopes, our desires, our fears, and our prejudices. Jesus cleared a way through all this. His disciples came to believe that God, the mysterious Presence that holds us in existence, is Love (*1 John 4:16*). Well, that is the best word that Jesus' disciples could come up with to speak of God as revealed by Jesus. To love is to give oneself to another. Jesus' disciples came to see that the universe is God's Self-gift. No wonder we look for love and seek to know more so that we can be in deeper communion.

We do not experience God as an object, but we know that the existence we experience is dependent on so many things, but ultimately on God (*see page 3*). We experience the universe as sacred. When we choose to 'believe' this (when we choose to 'be' in this 'love' that sustains us in existence), we believe in God as Jesus believed in God, and we live in gratitude to Jesus who shows us this amazing truth: that God, the Gracious Presence who is the sustaining source of everything, is Love.

Sharing Jesus' faith includes an attraction to get to know Jesus better, to listen to his words and watch his way of relating to people. He believed in God as Love and his disciples came to believe that everything Jesus was and everything he said and did flows from the intimate communion he experiences with the One whom he and his contemporaries called God. Paul speaks of the fruit of this communion:

> The fruit of the Spirit is love, joy, peace, patience kindness, generosity, faithfulness, gentleness and self-control (*Galatians 5:22*).

Paul was convinced that 'neither death, nor life, nor angels, nor rulers, nor things present, nor things to come ... nor anything else in all creation, will be able to separate us from the love of God in the Messiah Jesus, our Lord' (*Romans 8:38-39*).

Relating to God is fundamentally and necessarily an experience of myself, the knowing subject, as receiving existence, and as being loved and inspired. When we pause to enjoy communing with nature (a grove of trees, a spring, a mountain, the moon), we sense a sacred presence that draws us to the heart of nature, and at the same time mysteriously transcends what we are experiencing. This is especially so in a loving personal relationship. We find ourselves, to some degree, in communion with God.

Jesus wants us to share in his experience of being loved, and in the God who he believes is loving and inspiring him. Jesus draws people into this experience, an experience that is already happening in the core of our being, but we do not dare to believe it till he encourages us by the example and the gift of his love. For Jesus, God is the source of all he is. God is Self-giving love. No wonder Jesus is open to everyone. No wonder he believes in people. He knows that he is loved, and he knows that this is true for everyone. We don't have to change our lives to be loved by God. Of course, we want to change our lives, for we want to 'live to the full' (*John 10:10*), but this is not a pre-requisite for being loved by God. Quite the contrary, it is God's love that offers us the grace to change, if we would only believe in God's love and welcome it.

If by the word 'God' we mean the God that Jesus reveals, we have to make space in our lives to reflect on what we really long for. We want to belong. We want to be at home in the universe. We want to be in communion with God, which is to say communion with the Gracious Mystery that is at the heart of everything and everyone. God is what we all share. We belong to each other. We are one with the universe. Everything is a radiance of God. Jesus believes this. Any God who is less than this is not yet truly the God who sustains us in existence.

We conclude this section with two poems by James McAuley, one of Australia's leading lyric poets.

> Though all men should desert you my faith shall not grow less,
> but keep that single virtue of simple thankfulness.
> Pursuit had closed around me. Terrors had pressed me low.
> You sought me and you found me, and I will not let you go.
>
> The hearts of men grow colder, the final things draw near.
> Forms vanish, kingdoms moulder, the antirealm is here
> whose order is derangement: close-driven, yet alone,
> men reach the last estrangement, the sense of nature gone.
>
> Though the stars run distracted,
> and from wounds deep rancours flow,
> while the mystery is enacted I will not let you go.
> *Collected poems 1934-1970*, Angus and Robertson 1971

Shortly before his death from cancer, when all his life-springs were running dry, McAuley wrote:

> I know that faith is like a root that's tough, inert and old.
> Yet it can send up its green shoot and flower against the cold.
> I know there is a grace that flows when all the springs run dry.
> It wells up to renew the rose and lift the cedars high.

2. Experiencing love is experiencing God

It is common for people to imagine God as another object featuring in the list of objects that we seek to experience, understand, and define. Such a way of imagining God necessarily limits God. A finite God makes no sense. God transcends everything we experience and cannot be identified with any object that comes within our experience. This transcendent God is also immanent: sustaining everything in existence. Is this not what we mean when we speak of creation and of God as Creator?

To the question 'Do we experience God?' we can share Jesus' faith by replying that we experience God whenever we experience love. God is not another being, another person, who becomes another object we can experience and locate and come to know. Everything we know is relevant to our building up our understanding of God. What we experience and come to know draws us increasingly to being in love. From his own experience and understanding, Jesus came to believe that in experiencing love he was experiencing God. That is what he taught us. That is what his disciples came to call the 'good news'.

However complicated our lives can be, however overwhelming the hurts we receive from others, and however we may fail to love others, there is a Being whose loving accounts for our existing and sustains us. We human beings know this when we experience the attraction that draws us to receive love, and to reach out to give ourselves to others in love. Every creature is a word of God, yearning and striving to transcend itself and evolve so as to be in closer communion with its Creator. Evolution is often fragmentary, provisional, inconsistent. Much that we observe is random, but choosing to believe in God is a more reasonable choice than choosing not to believe in God. If there is no God, there is no meaning. Where does that leave us?

3. Coming to know God

Coming to 'know' God is a journey that never ends. It is a journey in which we are to be open to everything, and open in love. Whenever we experience receiving love, we are experiencing God. Whenever we reach out to anything or anyone in the giving of ourselves in love, we are experiencing God. Everything has its origin in God, in God's Word: 'let it be'. Everything is an expression of the outpouring of God's Spirit. God's Self-giving enables our self-giving.

The whole of creation exists because it is a finite participation in the very being of God. Everything is an expression (a limited, imperfect, but real expression) of God. Everything belongs because everything is held in existence by, and gives expression to, the one God. Seeing Jesus as the Word of God in human form reminds us to listen to all the ways God speaks to us. Watching Jesus inspired by God reminds us to wonder at the way God pours God's life-giving Spirit into each of us, embracing us in love and drawing us into communion.

In a mysterious way, everything is graced to be divine. Everything that God speaks, everything God wills into being, is an expression of God, a revelation of God. Everything comes from God, and longing to be in a more intimate communion with its source (with God) everything looks to God. In the words of the Beloved Disciple: 'The Word (the spoken word: creation) was towards [Greek *'pros'*] God' (*John 1:1*).

The Beloved Disciple continues: 'All things came into being through the Word. Without the Word not one thing came into being' (*John 1:3*). The author of Genesis speaks of light coming into existence because of God's Word: 'Let there be light!' Genesis speaks of light, the sky, the earth and the sea, the birds, the animals, and the fish. These are all created expressions of God. The inspired author reaches the climax when he has God say: 'Let us make humankind in our own image, according to our likeness' (*Genesis 1:3-27*).

Creatures do not add to God. We don't have God and then all these creatures that are not God. Such a God would be too small. When we speak of God, we are speaking of the mysterious, sustaining, gracious Presence at the heart of each created being, a Presence that holds everything in existence and that is revealing in each existing reality an aspect of the divine. We are speaking of God 'in whom we live and move and have our being' (Acts 17:28).

4. Of his fulness we have all received

'What has come into being in the Word was life, and life was the light of all people' (*John 1:4*). Focusing on life, John introduces

Jesus: *'The Word became flesh and lived among us, and we have seen his glory, the glory as of a father's only son, full of grace and truth'* (*John 1:14*). The divine Word is expressed in every creature, nowhere more clearly, more beautifully, more astonishingly for us than in the person of Jesus. This is what identifies Christianity. To come to know God, we need to be open to all creation. God's Word tells us to keep our eyes on Jesus if we are to see creation for what it is. It is the experience of being in communion with Jesus, of sharing in Jesus' intimacy with God, that enables us to go to the heart of everything and see there a reflection of God: *'From his fulness we have all received, grace upon grace'* (*John 1:16*). By way of conclusion, the evangelist reminds us: *'No one has ever seen God. It is the only Son who is in the bosom of the Father who has made God known'* (*John 1:18*).

We cannot directly experience or know God, but everything we experience reveals something of the One 'in whom we live and move and have our being' (*Acts 17:28*). We cannot over-estimate the gift that Jesus of Nazareth gave us in revealing God as Love. To see where God is in any situation, we are to look for love, for one being giving itself to another. Where we see love, we see God.

Psalm 67:1

Let us reflect on the opening words of Psalm 67: 'O God, be gracious and bless us'. What does it mean to ask God to be gracious? The God revealed by Jesus cannot be anything else. It is God who is holding us in being instant by instant of our existence. If that were not the case, we would simply cease to be. Aware of the precarious nature of our life, the author of Genesis speaks of us being formed by God out of the surface dust of the earth. Just imagine what would happen if God, the potter, were to withdraw his hands! We hold together only because God continues to hold us and embrace us in care. We are alive because God continues to breathe into us the breath of life.

In asking God to be gracious, we are really encouraging each other to remember who we are, so that we will remember who it is that is holding us in existence, and allow ourselves to be held and embraced, so that we will not forget to breathe in, as it were, and know where our life is coming from. We are invited by Jesus to believe that our life is coming from God.   But that is not all. Not only is God holding each of us in existence now, and giving us life now, God is also inviting us to share in the Love that is the Father, the Lover that is the Son, the Loving that is the Spirit. John has Jesus say at the Last Supper: 'If you love me, you will keep my word, and my Father will love you, and we will come to you and make our home with you' (*John 14:23, 27*).

When we ask God to be gracious, we are not asking God to keep on offering us this intimate communion. It is of the very nature of God to keep offering love. Nothing we have ever done, nothing we could ever do, could change that. What we are asking is that we might remember this offering and open our hearts to receive it and keep on opening ourselves to be loved. The key is to believe this even when our circumstances incline us to forget it and to give up hope.   We are tempted to try to secure our own happiness independent of our reliance on God, forgetting Jesus' warning that if we seek to secure our own life, we will lose it (*Mark*

8:35). Sometimes, other people treat us badly and we feel not accepted and cheated, and we lose hope in the value of our lives. We watch Jesus on the cross, but it is not easy to learn the lesson that what other people do or do not do to us cannot separate us from God's love. What they did to Jesus could not separate him from that love. We are graced to share Jesus' faith. There is a lot of pain in our lives. Some of it is caused by the failure of others, even those closest to us, who fail to know us, trust us and love us. Some of it is caused by our own failures. Pain is pain and it cannot be wished away. If we forget who we are as creatures of God, and if we forget that God is inviting us to share in God's life of love even in the midst of life's suffering, then pain can drive us to despair, or to behaviour that compounds the situation and wedges us further and further into the mess.

If we remember that God is holding us in existence, that God is always present in every circumstance, gracing us, supporting us, and holding us in love, then we will be able to look for the grace that is present and draw strength from it to cope and to grow in love even in the most trying of circumstances. When we ask God to be gracious, we are reminding ourselves of God's love and directing our attention to draw on the grace that is certainly always present. Psalm 67:1 continues: 'Let your face shed its light upon us'. This touches upon our deepest need. We are made for God and our hearts are restless till they rest in God. We are made by love and for love and the only love that can satisfy our desire is the experience of communion with God. All the loves that we experience here are necessarily fragile and imperfect, for we are all only learning to love, and we can all fail. We can fail. God cannot fail and God is love. 'Nothing can separate us from the love of God in Jesus' (*Romans 8:39*).

Saint Anselm: Archbishop of Canterbury (d.1109)

Come now, fly for a moment from your affairs,
escape for a little while from the tumult of your thoughts.
Put aside now your weighty cares and leave your wearisome toils.
Abandon yourself for a little to God and rest for a little in God.
Enter into the inner chamber of your soul, shut out everything
save God and what can be of help in your quest for God,
and, having locked the door, seek God out.

Speak now my whole heart, speak now to God:
'I seek your face, O Lord, your face I seek.' ...
What shall I do, most high God, what shall this exile do,
tormented by love of you and yet cast off far from your face?
I yearn to see you, I desire to come close to you, I long to find you,
I am eager to seek you out and I do not see your face ...
Look upon us, Lord; hear us, enlighten us, show yourself to us.
Give yourself to us that it may be well with us,
for without you it goes so ill for us.

Have pity on our efforts and our strivings towards you,
for we can avail nothing without you.
Teach me to seek you, and reveal yourself to me as I seek,
because I can neither seek you if you do not teach me how,
nor find you unless you reveal yourself.
Let me seek you in desiring you;
let me desire you in seeking you;
let me find you in loving you;
let me love you in finding you. (*Proslogion online Chapter 1*)

Paul to the Galatians 2:20

It is no longer I who live. It is Christ who lives in me. The life I now live I live by the faith of the Son of God, loving me, giving himself for me.

www.ingramcontent.com/pod-product-compliance
Lightning Source LLC
Chambersburg PA
CBHW012006090526
44590CB00026B/3903